A Second Classroom

"What Torin has so sensitively crafted here will give you greater simplicity and spaciousness in school community life. I highly recommend this book to all parents and teachers, but especially to those connected to Waldorf schools."

—**Kim John Payne,** M.Ed., author of *Simplicity Parenting* and *Beyond Winning*

"This book is a call for parents and teachers to work more effectively together on behalf of our children. Torin uses a variety of approaches to stimulate conversation and help us strengthen the communities around our schools. I highly recommend this provocative book!"

—**David Sobel,** author of *Place-Based Education: Connecting Classrooms and Communities*

A SECOND CLASSROOM

*Parent–Teacher Relationships
in a Waldorf School*

TORIN M. FINSER, PhD

STEINERBOOKS | 2014

STEINERBOOKS
AN IMPRINT OF ANTHROPOSOPHIC PRESS, INC.
610 Main St., Great Barrington, MA 01230
www.steinerbooks.org

Book design by William Jens Jensen
Cover image by John Beck:
Threefold foundation Auditorium,
Chestnut Ridge, NY

"Reading the Face" in the appendices is from the book *Reading the Face:
Understanding a Person's Character through Physiognomy* by Norbert Glas
(Temple Lodge Press, 2008); used by kind permission of the publisher.

PUBLICATION OF THIS WORK WAS MADE POSSIBLE

BY A GRANT FROM THE WALDORF CURRICULUM FUND.

LIBRARY OF CONGRESS CONTROL NUMBER: 2014933148
ISBN: 978-1-62148-063-1 (paperback)
ISBN: 978-1-62148-064-8 (ebook)

Contents

DEDICATION

This book is dedicated to the mothers and fathers of today who bring to life the children who will guide and lead our world to a better future. Our schools are an expression of hope for the future of humanity. In particular, I would like to dedicate this book to two sets of parents without whom Karine and I would not be here:

Lise and Jorn M. Jensen, mother and father of Karine, Anne, Jesper.

Ruth and Siegfried E. Finser, mother and father of Torin, Mark, Angela.

Together they have seen the birth and growth of 13 grandchildren.

Acknowledgements

More so than with my previous books, this work has been a team effort, from the alum who helped give birth to the title to the many parents and teachers who participated in the survey and interviews. I would like to thank the Waldorf schools that supported the distribution of the survey (Portland Waldorf School, Waldorf School on the Roaring Forks, Cincinnati Waldorf School, Pine Hill and Monadnock Waldorf School and the work-study students and volunteers who helped collate the survey. I am once again ever so grateful to Nicky Wheeler-Nicholson for her impeccable editing, now with all the latest benefits of up-to-date software, and to SteinerBooks for agreeing to publish this book. Although there are larger publishing houses out there with significant marketing budgets, I remain committed to small independent publishers and local bookstores. They deserve our full-hearted support for the sake of academic and cultural freedom, as well as the availability of a wide spectrum of published material in hard copy and ebooks. May we never forget that freedom of choice is the foundation of democracy.

Preface

The inspiration for this book was sparked during a conversation at the Thai Restaurant on Main Street in Keene, New Hampshire. I was talking with a former student, who was describing her impressions of parent–teacher work in Waldorf schools. During our conversation, she said, "It is almost as if the teacher today needs a second classroom, given the importance of working with parents." This immediately lit up a long-standing theme in my work, including topics I covered in two courses at Antioch, the one on administration and the other on organizational integrity. We discussed the idea of a book on this topic and the possibility of offering a new course that could be taught jointly by a parent and a teacher. This then led to my sending a proposal to my publisher and the launch of a new project.

Many know of the unusual response Rudolf Steiner gave to the question, "What is the ideal class size?" He responded by saying, "How many parents can you work with?" Even though this exchange occurred almost a hundred years ago, it serves as a ringing endorsement for this book, in that it places parent–teacher work as a high priority for our schools, especially those that rely on parent volunteerism to survive.

There are several additional justifications for this work: Many of our alums from teacher education programs report that although they were mostly well prepared for curriculum design, working with children in age appropriate ways and a host of other key attributes to good teaching, they were not ready for the challenges in working with parents. Even those who had a course or two that covered the topic, as we do at Antioch, reported that the theme did not really hit home until they were in charge of a group of children and actually immersed in the work. The preparatory work seemed theoretical to them at the time, and they were not able to fully understand the issues until they were working with real parents in day-to-day interactions in schools.

There has also been a host of studies showing that student success in schools depends significantly on parent participation in their schools. Actively engaged parents who help with homework, go on field trips, attend class nights, and so on stimulate positive learning in their children and the teacher is more engaged. In contrast, passivity can lead to disengagement and lower student achievement. In short, healthy parent–teacher and parent–school relations can make a huge difference in our children's lives.

We have all heard horror stories about things that have gone wrong. When a relationship breaks down, it can lead to relocation, loss of friends, and family disruption. Independent schools can suffer loss of enrollment that affects financial viability; public schools can suffer in terms of reputation and standing in the community when parent dissatisfaction grows. It is in the best interests of all concerned that the adult relationships in a school model community and healthy social interaction.

Through surveys and interviews, I was able to capture stories and share case studies that illustrate the challenges of parent–teacher work. Some of the topics I raise in this book have long been considered taboo. I raise them here not to judge (at some points the reader may feel I am pro-parent, at others pro-teacher), but to make these issues acceptable for discussion. Unless they are looked at openly and honestly, we cannot improve. It is hoped that we can learn from these experiences and not be compelled to repeat past mistakes. We can learn from one another.

Finally, it takes a great leap of faith for a person to enter the teaching profession these days. This book outlines some "best practices," directed especially toward beginning teachers to help them get off to a good start. Included are a variety of practical, common-sense suggestions that can support successful parent–teacher interactions. This book is intended to help parents and teachers collaborate for the benefit of the children.

As adults, we are looked to as role models. Children see and observe more than we often give them credit for, and what they see shapes their attitudes toward adulthood. How parents and teachers work together can go a long way toward shaping future relationships. Our world needs more attention to communication, meeting mutual needs, problem solving, group work and a host of other skills that can be fostered in the context of a school as a learning organization for all involved. How the adults work together can be as important as the curriculum on any given day. Yet we need to do this work jointly; it takes two to tango!

We often get stuck in the ways we frame issues and cling to old views of one another. Catch phrases such as "hysterical parents" and "controlling teachers" take on a life of their own. We need to move beyond the slogans and develop new self-awareness. This book brings a wide variety of perspectives so that we—parents, teachers, administrators, and friends of education—can look at ourselves and grow from the experience. It is no longer enough simply to have a few potluck picnics and think we are dealing with the social issues of a school. What is really needed is meaningful work together, and that work is all about developing community.

Finally, the practical advice contained in this book (thanks to the many respondents to surveys and interviews) is augmented by some philosophical aspects intended to stimulate deeper reflection. Thus the reader will find chapters on "I–thou" and "I–it," increasing and decreasing, family of origin, and so on. While not exhaustive on the subject, the intention is to give birth to new perspectives that make it increasingly likely that both parents and teachers self-observe. When we become self-aware, we are more likely to fight our inner battles first. There may be less need to "play things out" externally if we have done inner work ahead of time. With a few exceptions, the chapters in this book alternate between practical advice and inner dimensions.

As with most things in life, the outer challenges are often accompanied by inner struggles. Thus this book has been organized along two, concurrent lines: practical skills and the inner journey. The former will take up the presenting issues and work with them in a direct, common-sense way, with emphasis on applications. The second strand will look at some of the same issues and others from a deeper, more philosophical point of view. The outer path chapters will be in a regular font, the inner path sections will be in italics. One could read the chapters in sequence or follow a particular strand by skipping sections; it is the reader's choice.

My hope is that this book serves and inspires. In the end, it is all about our children; they hold the keys to our future.

Words of Advice

Part 1: For the Beginning Teacher

It seems like just a short time ago that I was a true beginning teacher, although the start of each school year still brings a small echo of that original feeling. I was 22 years old, idealistic, naïve, and ever so eager to do things right. Most of my prep time was spent on the curriculum, although I did do home visits and interviewed other teachers regarding the children I was about to inherit. Looking back on my first weeks, I am reminded of the phrase, "But for the grace of God..." how did I ever manage?

Many of the parents in my first class were old enough to be my biological parents. Some of them tried to give me advice, some were truly puzzled, and others probably wondered if I would last. But most of all, they were kind and understanding. When I struggled with a boy who was easily frustrated, his dad, a plant manager locally, quietly explained that his son was the same way at home, and that all he needed was some "time out" in between assignments. Another mother helped me understand that her daughter was very conscious of her Jewish identity and often burst into tears at any injustice. It seemed at times as if the parents "took me on" just as seriously as I had taken on their children.

This led to an early but powerful lesson in the parent–teacher relationship:

Parents truly want teachers to succeed, and are willing to go to extraordinary lengths to make that possible.

In the thirty-five years since, I have learned a great deal from the teacher perspective and I have continued to learn through the eyes of colleagues still in the classroom and our Antioch interns. As a result, I would like to share some advice for the beginning teacher:

Build relationships from day one. The parents are just as important as their children, and one ignores them at one's peril. Get to know them, ask questions, visit their homes, learn about their professions, where they were born and their major life events. Information can lead to knowledge, and if processed well, knowledge can lead to the exercise of wisdom.

As part of building relationships, practice it regularly: parent evenings, parent conferences, phone calls home, etc. If the communication is regular, one can catch issues early on before they become "problems." (See more on conflict in chapter 12 and some very interesting results in the survey chapter later.)

Keep accurate records. I had a separate folder/notebook for each family, in which I included copies of my year-end reports, notes from parent–teacher conferences and dates and times of phone calls. This helped me avoid the obvious embarrassment of contradicting myself, and allowed me to glance quickly at the history of the relationship prior to a new conversation. One year a mother said, "You have been out of touch with us." I then quietly recited the dates of our interactions over the past year, to which she could not find a response and changed the subject. Here was another lesson for me:

Parents often speak out of their perceptions of reality. Those perceptions, when guided more by feeling than external reality, need to be dealt with. Otherwise, they take on a life of their own.

In a wonderful interview with Eugene Schwartz, he described his "crisis-proof" way of working with parents. He would call each family twice per month, in addition to normal class nights and conferences. But those calls were based on a vigorous process:

He would observe the child (or three at a time) with extra attention in school.

Eugene then would call the parents to share an upbeat story or anecdote, and then ask the parent how the child was doing at home.

He would end by asking the parent how she/he was doing; reference their last conversation about the job change, family loss or other topic.

Eugene also strenuously avoided talking substance in accidental meetings at the supermarket, etc. Social events were purely social, no mixing business with pleasure. And Eugene had much to say about dads.

Work with dads and well as moms. Just as most early-childhood and elementary teachers tend to be women, it is the same with parental participation. More moms tend to show up at school events. A teacher should never ignore dads. One of my graduate students once did a paper on working with dads in which she discovered that many of the things we routinely do in a Waldorf school offended dads, because they notice things, and some things have more meaning for them than others. My grad student reported that dads were particularly put off by such things as poor maintenance of the physical plant, flowery communication that did not get to the point, inconsistencies in communications, and school policies (one teacher allowing one kind of T-shirt, another not allowing it). Eugene said he tried to make at least one joke or share an anecdote about business, politics, or sports each class night.

Always respect the choices parents make for their homes. As teachers, we are in charge of many things all day long, and we may seem to be fully in charge of the children in our care. In fact, we are only temporary guardians during the day, as parents are legally and morally the main decision makers in the lives of their children. Parents make choices, some of which we may disagree with, but other than describing the affects on school life, we cannot sit in judgment or try to overrule parents on the home front. As a teacher, I have often had to remind myself that that child has chosen those parents (as seen from an Anthroposophical point of view), and no teacher can play God. We can ask questions, but we cannot over-rule. If parents feel disrespected or judged, they may reciprocate.

Treat parents as you would like to be treated. Open-mindedness and positivity work both ways.

Share your enthusiasm for teaching and for their children. En-theos, enthusiasm, is a spiritual, highly contagious condition. If you are excited about a lesson, science experiment or math discovery, share it! One of my teachers, Lee Lecraw, was so excited about botany and the Fibonacci series that I can still see her in my mind's eye counting the spirals on pine cones, flowers, shells. She became the subject and we were all swept along. This kind of true enthusiasm builds a sense of shared experience, of "being-with" that then transfers to other areas of the parent–teacher relationship.

Ask before stating. So often my blunders have been based on misinformation or my presumption of what a parent was thinking. Even if you think you know, it never hurts to ask again. Parents process things over time just as teachers do, and they may have moved on with an issue. Ask before telling. So for example, when following up on a parent–teacher conference, it might help to ask first, "Have you had a chance to give this more thought? How are you doing with my suggestions?"

Don't ever violate a parent's confidence by speaking of another family or child to a parent. If you want parents to trust you, be trustworthy. This becomes very difficult, however, when multiple adults are responsible for the same child, such as ex-spouses and new partners. I suggest asking those responsible how they want to handle matters. Unless there are court orders or legal restraints that indicate otherwise, go with the wishes of those most directly responsible for the daily care of the child in question. But with weekend visitations and grandparent caregivers and such it can become very complicated. Nonetheless, I would still place a premium on trust-building, care, and tact regarding what is shared.

Trust is a commodity that takes time to earn and is easily lost. Trust and confidence are an invisible yet powerful currency in any relationship—its value rises and falls as with other currencies, yet when it is highly valued, it has positive effects on many other spheres of interaction.

Enjoy and respect the parents of your students. They are worth getting to know, and they can bring the world to your doorstep if you are willing to see the treasures they offer. The parents of your students are a microcosm of the world as a whole, with all its diversity, cultural heritage, knowledge and shared experiences, both good and not so good. It is all there. Complaining about one parent or another is to show your lack of understanding of this human riddle:

The parents a teacher works with often represent the next step in relational development for the teacher as a person. These wonderful people (parents) represent an implicit invitation to grow as a person not just as a teacher. Accept the invitation or you can be sure to receive many more invites in the future. What we do not accept as a task today may simply come back at us again and again until we engage.

Finally, I urge the motivated reader to look at the survey results in the appendices under the question: What qualities in a teacher make for good parent interaction? In addition to the expected responses such as empathy, listening, availability, the parents surveyed offered some interesting insights on what makes for good relations from their perspective. And as we all know, seeing things from different perspectives goes a long way toward creating a healthy social life around a school.

Part 2: For New Parents

My oldest son, Thomas, started nursery school in 1985. Since then I have been a continuous parent of a school age child, a stretch of almost 30 years. When our youngest, Ionas graduates high school in 2018, it will have been 36 years! I have learned more along the way than in any course or degree. Parenting has had a profound effect on my life, and continues to do so, as even the older ones continue to turn homeward for advice and support from time to time. Once a parent, always a parent.

Contrary to popular assumptions, our children have attended a variety of schools due to moves, their needs, and changes in staff. The basis for giving advice below is based upon parenting experience at the following schools: Great Barrington Rudolf Steiner School, Pine Hill, High Mowing, The Well School (a non-Waldorf private school), Conval (a secondary public school), Northfield Mount Hermon, and Monadnock Waldorf School. Each of these eight schools treated parents differently, and in some cases, such as Pine Hill, we were returning parents as Thomas, Ewen and Louisa attended during one era and then some years later Ionas attended grades K-5. Likewise with Monadnock Waldorf. Not surprisingly, schools change over time. Yet at the same time (and contradictions are okay) each school has its own particular Being, or presence, that can last over generations. Thus although my father graduated from High Mowing in the fifties, our children experienced many of the same traditions and qualities that he did. Matching a child with a school is a high art form, a subject perhaps for another book.

Having given previous advice for the starting teacher, here are some pointers for parents beginning the journey with school-aged children:

Practice conscious trust. Parents want to know that their children are learning, safe, and loved, and if you have confidence in your child's teacher extend your trust, for the teacher needs space in which to work. That trust cannot be blind, it must be conscious. That means engaging in dialogue when needed, following up on issues, but then backing off again when something is resolved. Parents need to give teachers space for growth and development within reasonable bounds. This is conscious trust.

Attend events, from parent evenings to conferences to school assemblies and special events. There is no substitute for participation. These events can be lots of fun, and you may develop wonderful parent-to-parent connections and even friendships. And if you have an observing eye, you can learn a lot about how a school works, what makes people "tick" and how teachers interact with each other by being an observer/participant. Then when you ask questions, you have a context, a base of experience.

Parents, please participate to the fullest extent possible. Watch for those feelings of guilt when you cannot measure up to your expectations or participate as much as you would like. So many parents today have to work long hours, even multiple jobs, and one can soon develop feelings of inadequacy. This has a corrosive effect, sometimes turning into negativity that can burst out around an issue that might otherwise be dealt with easily. It helps to tell your child's teacher at the beginning of the year about your circumstances and what you can and cannot do. Most teachers I know are very understanding. Set up a communication buddy system with another parent so you can get updates, and read your emails and notices from the school. Choose a few events to attend and make the most of them (not everything at the school is of equal importance).

Communicate frequently. Teachers, though frequently good observers, are usually not mind readers. They need to know what is going on. A note, email, or phone call can go a long way toward keeping them posted. Most questions and issues can be resolved quickly. It is only when things are left unattended that we tend to get into conflict. Catch things early on.

You will be stretched (as will the teachers!). You may experience incredible joy in witnessing your child's progress, seeing the projects that are brought home, and hearing the many stories of school. You will also be challenged, as there will be things that push you out of your usual comfort zone. Most parents have developed professional expertise in the workplace and many exude competence. Yet when it comes to school relations, parents are not in control. Processes and procedures used in the workplace may not be evident at the school. Some things may even defy common sense. This can be unnerving. As a parent, I often felt like a piece of driftwood at sea, not sure of my bearings. This adjustment can be challenging.

Manage your expectations and disappointments. Particularly in the beginning of a relationship to a new school, expectations can soar. This is the so-called honeymoon period, often most evident among parents of young children. Then one realizes that teachers are human beings too, and no one is perfect. (See more on this theme in chapter 16 on the life cycle of parent involvement.) In my experience, most teachers are sincerely striving, and parents can do a lot to encourage teachers through expressions of appreciation. What is it that holds us all together?

Goodwill is the foundation of successful parent–teacher relationships. Parents influence each other. This can be supportive in sharing tips on child rearing, commiserating, networking with community groups, and after-school activities. Or this can turn negative as in gossip clubs and favoring some children over others. Who do you invite to birthday parties? How will you handle challenging social situations among the children? When one of our children entered a new school halfway through first grade one of the parents told us, "There is only one child left—all the others (25 children) are taken and already have best friends." No one extended invitations for play dates, and sure enough, everyone else was in a clique. And all this in first grade! A footnote: 16 years later, long after high school and well into the college years, one of those girls called our daughter to apologize for what they had all done to her years before.

Parents are jointly responsible for the social health of the group. At an Association of Waldorf Schools of North America (AWSNA) conference many years ago, Dave Alsop, then chair of the organization, gave a talk in which he said, "Parents have angels, too." With this simple comment he indicated a basic truth: all of us are striving human beings with a spiritual life, whether we take it up consciously or not. The teachers do not have a lock on self-development and personal growth. Parents can work together in study groups, take on topics of interest together and become a learning community. Much as we respect and appreciate our teachers, we need to respect the expertise and humanity of our fellow parents. How we work together serves as a role model for our children.

We need to work on both our welcoming and our good-byes. Some schools have assigned welcoming parents to help with orientation, which is great. We are often less capable when it comes to saying good-bye. How about an exit interview? And will other parents call to say good-bye, or is there just a deafening silence?

Our humanity is revealed in the in-between moments of life, and saying good-bye is one of them. The path of parenting is one of heart-warming love and continual sacrifice. Nothing in life prepared me for raising children and situations such as a sick child in the middle of the night, homework tantrums, teenage moodiness, or talking back. This path of parenting is a modern path of initiation; we grow tremendously as a result of our love and sacrifices. In the end, it is worth every minute. There is a tenderness and intimacy that is irreplaceable. And herein lies one last riddle: the relationship of a parent to his/her child will always be different than that of a teacher to the same child. We want our children to be seen and understood, but it will never be as deep as the subterranean current between a parent and child. That is as it should be. Yet our love comes with a large dose of subjectivity.

Teachers can help us see our children
from different points of view and
can help bring objectivity

2

Self-less-ness

*I*n my book, Finding Your Self, *I described a path of inner development that can lead to a greater realization of one's Self, a journey toward identity. The path of contemplation leads the meditant toward heightened self-awareness and expanded consciousness. In the exercises given, there are many opportunities to grow both personally and professionally. This is not just a matter of self-actualization as so many "New Age" groups would maintain, but really a call for finding one's inner core as a human being and thus being in a position to better serve the universal human in others.*[1]

As indicated in How to Know Higher Worlds *and many other places, Rudolf Steiner asserts that one has to take three steps in the development of one's moral character for everyone in self-development. If one does not, harmful influences present in all of us can actually grow stronger. One can become even more self-centered, self-seeking, only now with a veneer of spirituality. To put it bluntly, there is nothing worse than a self-righteous person who has adopted the language of spirituality but has not made any inner changes (see the chapter, "Finding One's Inner Core in Finding Your Self").*

One of the greatest challenges faced by human beings today, parents and teachers included, is that of selfishness. It is a malady of our time. As part of our hard-won victory to become free human beings through a long evolution of consciousness, we have arrived

---

1   See my book, *Finding Your Self* (published by AWSNA).

at a place where we stand as individuals firmly on the Earth. We can either lift our gaze to see the stars (or the wonders of humanity around us), or we can focus only on ourselves. Thanks to rampant materialism, many choose a self-centered approach: my nutrition, my exercise routine, my retreats, my self-help books, my needs for…all of which, though well intended, can lead to a kind of spiritual materialism.

One of the basic challenges of parent–teacher relations is in overcoming selfishness. Both parties suffer from it. For the teacher, it can be an emphasis on following personal inclinations in preparation and thus teaching what one most likes to teach, or postponing tasks that are more difficult. Although perfectly understandable, a teacher can guard his or her personal space too strongly and be unapproachable. Some might be reluctant to serve on committees or take up school-wide responsibilities. Parents also struggle with selfishness, after all it is their child in question, and their family is at stake. Parents can easily fall into single-issue advocacy, forgetting that there are many dimensions to learning. Parents often want action, now, today, and can forget that there are other children in a class that also deserve the teacher's attention. Although one might argue with my examples, it would be hard to refute the fact that both parents and teachers have to contend with the tug of selfishness, and that self-seeking can pull us apart.

So what can we do? There are many places to start, but one that serves in a timeless way is that path of letting go, of shedding the snakeskin. (See note at end of this chapter for more on shedding the snakeskin from the perspective of other cultures.) One such pathway comes to us through ancient teachings and the well-known phrase "He must increase; I must decrease."

These words of St. John ring forth through the centuries of time in their seeming simplicity, yet they have momentous implications for all who take them to heart. Who is it that must increase? It is the One, the Christ, who for the longest time was felt with such shattering impact of soul that His name would not *even be spoken. Who is it that must decrease? It is John, the one who came before, the one who assisted in the baptism of new life. The reality of these simple words represent not just a biblical or historical event, they continue to live on in a continuing drama of human life on this Earth.*

Human beings today live at the crossroad of two realities: on the one hand, the descent into Selfhood has given us unprecedented freedom. We are able to think, feel and will out of our own resolution, independent of the cosmos. This freedom today has resulted in much technological achievement. On the other hand, each human being has a Spirit Self that visits a physical body during a lifetime on Earth. This spiritual core is the lifeline to the past and to the wider cosmos. It is a lifeline to the eternal.

In a passage known as "Credo," written at the young age of 27, Rudolf Steiner said, "The individual must have Spirit in its own self, lest it drop off, like a dry leaf, from the Tree of Creation, having existed in vain."[2] What a wonderful image! Without the Spirit, the individual is like a dry leaf! Just as we move from one lifetime to another, so the leaves on the Tree of Life come and go. What is essential and eternal is the tree, which has living sap, growth, and the ability to endure the passage of time.

So what is it in us that must decrease? We must work to diminish all that is selfish, all that calls on us to be finite, isolated beings, for this part of us tends to obscure the light of the spirit: "What springs from the impulses of sensuality, from desire and passion, is only what is craved by this egoistic individual. Therefore people must deaden this selfish willing within themselves; instead of willing what they desire as individuals, they must will what the Spirit, or Idea, wills within them. Abandon isolation and follow the voice of the Idea in yourself; for it alone is the Divine."

In this view of decreasing, the individual becomes a mere point on the circumference of the universe, a point that ultimately vanishes

---

2   Steiner, "Credo," 1.

in the stream of time. The Spirit is the center, the central light of the universe that shines forth; it cannot be defeated by time.

From Steiner's "St. John's Imagination," we have the words:

> *Spirit's high weaving,*
> *Radiance kindling,*
> *Warming life.*[3]

When working out of the spirit's high weaving, I can unite myself with universal world activity. Deadening, or decreasing "self-hood" in the everyday sense is the prescription for a higher life. "We are immortal to the degree in which we let this selfhood die in us."[4] Thus we can understand the true meaning of the old proverb, "Those who do not die before they die will perish when they die."[5] We have to let a part of ourselves fall away in order to participate in universal life. This is the secret to initiation.

So where and how can we "increase"? We can do this when we submit ourselves in loving devotion to the pursuit of the spirit. This can happen in a variety of ways, for example:

Through the seeking of knowledge we find devotion to the universe in thoughts.
Art can be seen as a kind of devotion to the universe in perception.
Religion is devotion to the universe in the heart.
Love is devotion to the sum-total of our spirit-forces to something that is worthy of our esteem.

Again from Steiner: "Knowledge is the most spiritual, Love the most beautiful form of selfless devotion. For Love is truly a light of Heaven in the life of an earthly day . . . it elevates everything that lives in us. This pure and reverent love transforms the life of the soul so that it becomes related to the Spirit of the Universe. . . . Those

---

3   Steiner, *The Four Seasons and the Archangels*, p. 54; "*Schaue unser Weben / das leuchtende Erre / das wärmende Leben.*"

4   Steiner, "Credo," 2.

5   Ibid.

who live in the Spirit live in freedom."[6] *Thus one has to lose oneself to find oneself in the Cosmic Spirit. One has to die to become. "He must increase, but I must decrease."*

In everyday life, these lofty realities are often experienced in small, in-between moments, yet often we do not notice them. There are countless times in a day in which one stands at the crossroad of selfhood (this is what I need or want to do now) and devotion to the Spirit (this is what calls me to step beyond myself). These moments are worth noticing, as they can be transformational. Great artists, painters, musicians, poets have woven their creations out of these transitional moments of human living. For example, our own New Englander, Robert Frost writes in his poem:

> *Stopping by Woods on a Snowy Evening*
> *Whose woods these are I think I know,*
> *His house is in the village though;*
> *He will not see me stopping here*
> *To watch his woods fill up with snow.*
>
> *My little horse must think it queer*
> *To stop without a farmhouse near*
> *Between the woods and frozen lake*
> *The darkest evening of the year.*
>
> *He gives his harness bells a shake*
> *To ask if there is some mistake,*
> *The only other sound's the sweep*
> *Of easy wind and downy flake.*
>
> *The woods are lovely, dark and deep.*
> *But I have promises to keep,*
> *And miles to go before I sleep,*
> *And miles to go before I sleep.*
>   *("Stopping by Woods on a Snowy Evening")*

---

6   Ibid.

It seems Frost wrote this poem in June 1922 while in Vermont. It was composed in just a few minutes early one morning, after having spent the whole night writing a long poem called New Hampshire. This in itself is revealing. It was an inspiration that passed through him, not the result of long cogitation. He was in a transition state of consciousness (early morning). There are many clues in the poem itself regarding this state of transition: the rider was "between" woods and frozen lake, the owner's house was in the village (the physical home) vs. the woods (trees as representing life forces). There is also the uncertainty of the horse shaking his harness bells.... The bells themselves often represent a call to service and a change in consciousness that can come with the sacrament. This poem is full of simple clues of the in-between state of consciousness we often find ourselves in, but instead of rushing on, Robert Frost paused for a moment to take it all in.

We all know the gentle scene of falling snow, a kind of blessing that covers all the sins of the world, if only temporarily. The woods become "lovely, dark and deep" in a winter landscape. So the soul can open to new depths if we but stop for a few moments now and then. Stopping by woods on a snowy evening is full of pictures that point to decreasing the rush of pounding hoofs of daily life to let the "increase" of soul-spirit fill us anew. The young Steiner ends his two-page "Credo" with a few simple words: "Let Truth become Life; lose yourself to find yourself in the cosmic Spirit."[7]

We can do this at any moment of the day. And we can do this through the arts. We can decrease, become less selfish, so that something new and living will increase within us. When we attend to the "increase," then there is a greater chance that the "promises we keep" will abide in our parent–teacher relationships.

---

7   Steiner, "Credo," 2.

It is your task in the Sun-hour
the tidings, wisdom filled, to recognize:
surrendered now to cosmic beauty,
to feel yourself in self, experience this:
the human "I" can lose itself
and find itself in cosmic "I."[8]

☙

NOTE ON SHEDDING A SNAKESKIN: The snake, or serpent, has appeared in many different cultures' mythology throughout history, symbolizing rebirth, transformation, immortality, and healing. In Chinese legends, The Queen of the West sits at the top of Snake Shaman Mountain and visits Earth on her chariot pulled by dragons to help human beings transcend ignorance and mortality. Similarly to the god Shiva in Hindu lore, the Queen of the West is known not only as the destroyer, but also the preserver and creator. Shiva is often depicted with snakes coiled around his neck while meditating at the top of his sacred mountain, representing tranquility and transcendence within a seemingly deadly situation. Both of these gods seek to aid humanity in recognizing that beneath the temporal nature of the flesh, the soul is eternal and can undergo infinite transformations and rebirths. Perhaps a more familiar version of this theme can be recognized in a symbol we see in our everyday lives in the staff of Asclepius, the ancient Greeks' god of medicine. Now the symbol for modern physicians, the intertwining snakes, which was the Greek's symbol of eternity, carry forth the hope of healing and rejuvenation.

---

8   Steiner, *Calendar of the Soul*, verse 11.

3

In Your Face

This common phrase masks an actual opportunity to understand better the people around us, including parents and teachers. Just as one can tell a Picasso from a Rembrandt, likewise human faces present opportunities to see the artist at work from within. In this chapter I will examine aspects of the human face from a three-fold point of view: thinking, feeling, and willing. After looking for external manifestations of these three aspects, the subsequent chapter will delve into soul/spiritual considerations.

When one meets someone for the first time, it is the face that often makes the first impression. One might connect with the eyes, a smile, or a distinctive expression. Taken as a whole, one can say that the face has three aspects:

The forehead may be high or low, creased or smooth, more or less rounded, and so on. A person who is perplexed or deep in thought might even draw the forehead together in furrows. In museums one can see the busts of great philosophers from the Greek or Roman era with pronounced foreheads. In other words, the forehead represents the human faculty of thinking.

The middle of the face features the eyes and nose. Here again, there is so much wonderful variety in human nature! We all know the power of the dark, silent eyes of a child or an adult's aristocratic nose. We, of course use the nose to inhale and exhale, a microcosm of what happens with the lungs in the exchange of air. This middle region of the face has to do with the rhythmic system and the human faculty of feeling.[1]

Then we have the mouth and chin. What a difference in the expression of a child who is pouting or smiling, laughing or weeping! Some people have strong, pronounced chins and others have chins that slope gently inward. We can see so much character in the lower portion of the face.

In his book, *Reading the Face: Understanding a Person's Character through Physiognomy,* Norbert Glas observes that in terms of human development, the forehead attains its final form early on in life, the middle portion of the face changes more thoroughly during life, and the chin, lips, and mouth require the most time to change over a lifetime. So if one compares photos of a person at various stages of life, one can see great continuity in the forehead, subtle changes in the middle region, and more pronounced changes in the chin and mouth area. We are shaped by life.

This is in contrast to the story of the human ear. What is most remarkable is that the ear changes hardly at all during the span of one lifetime. A child's outer ear is already fully developed, and remains virtually unchanged during life. Where does this remarkable form we call the ear come from? One could say it is a very old part of the human being, a symbol of the past. One could even say the ear is a picture of a past life. If we can learn to read these memorials of the past we can see more clearly what a person brings as gifts or weaknesses at birth. And an education truly dedicated to the child will try to help overcome hindrances so as to better take initiative in the present life.

Once again, one can understand the outer ear from a threefold aspect; the upper part is "head-like," in that through the helix (a, b, c in the diagram on page 20) the upper ear shows us the layout of the nerve-sense system, perceptive abilities, mental imagery, and thinking.

---

1   See www.well.blogs.nytimes.com/2013/10/03/well-quiz-the-mind-behind -the-eyes/?_r=1.

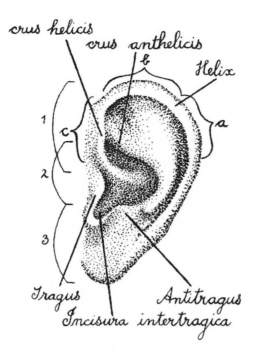

The middle area is an expression once again of the rhythmic part of the human being. It forms a cavity that leads down into the actual organ of hearing. Whereas the back is relatively undifferentiated, the *Crus helicis* in the front is a form with a dynamic curve dividing the cavity into two parts. The movement of breathing and blood circulation, which occur elsewhere in the body, are mirrored in this circular form. On the soul-level this movement, or circular form, signifies feeling.

The lower third of the outer ear represents the metabolic, the will system of the human being. Once again there are several parts— the button-like thickening (*Antitragus*) an incision point downward (*Incisura intertragica*), and the soft, fleshy ear lobe. This lower part of the auricle reveals the strength and force of the human will.[2]

---

2   Glas, *Reading the Face*, 23.

Thousands of years ago, the word for "ear" and for "wisdom" in the Sumerian language seems to have been one and the same. This word was probably *enki,* since the god of wisdom in Sumer was addressed by this name. "From the Great Above the goddess opened [set] her ear, her receptor for wisdom, to the Great Below."[3] If wisdom is conveyed through sound as well as sight, then singing, rhythmic gesture, and dance are included as its conveyors and amplifiers. Sound is powerful; sound can soothe, enlighten, inform, and stimulate. It challenges us with its potential, and we are dependent on our aural perception for the development of wisdom.

Norbert Glas and others have made extensive studies of the ear and other aspects of the human face, identifying mental, psychological, and character traits that make for a fascinating study (see appendices for a further example). The reader can look further into the literature on the subject if desired. But for the purposes of this book on parent–teacher relations, I will draw out the significance of the human face in our work together.

When we meet a person for the first time, our perceptions are often clouded by bits and pieces of information floating around inside of us: a comment someone made about that teacher, a previous encounter via phone or email, an impression shared by another family member. We often meet people in a state of suspended animation and with a cloud of subjectivity around us. We spend the first seconds or even minutes trying to inwardly prove or disprove these random bits of information. This can obscure our vision of whom we are actually meeting and detract from real observation.

Instead of the above, I would like to suggest a more phenomenological approach: quiet the bits of random information swirling around and simply observe. One can do this while still smiling, shaking hands, or exchanging pleasantries. But if one has schooled oneself in observation skills, much value can be gained by simply using one's eyes to actually observe. Even if the ears are covered over

---

3   Erikson, *The Life Cycle Completed,* 7.

by hair, one can still observe the forehead, nose, mouth, chin, and so on. Rather than going right into interpretation (this nose indicates a French person), I would simply stay with the phenomena without forming judgments and conclusions. Over time, one can then match these observations with actual experiences of the person:

> One has a large, rounded forehead. When I speak with that person, do I sometimes feel like I am with a philosopher?
> One's eyes smile even before the mouth does. Does this indicate a merry, lighthearted person?
> One's chin is very strong and firm. Do I later find out that this individual is a doer, a builder of stonewalls, or an acquisitions manager in business?

The question attached to each observation may over time be proven true or not, but the observation can hold fast. Our interpretations are usually more prone to error than the observations. Yet most of our lives are governed by interpretations. We need to ground ourselves again and again in the phenomena, for in the end, they will speak truly.

Observing the phenomena is also a discipline, as one has to ask again and again: what am I really seeing? What am I hearing? If one does that at several points in a parent–teacher conversation, it acts as a corrective, an anchor that pulls one back from hasty interpretation. One has to have the inner honesty to correct first impressions and let the phenomena speak. There will be more on this in the chapters on communication and conflict, but many of the social difficulties that occur between people are caused by premature interpretations and the holding of assumptions about one another.

Let's say, for example, that after much-tested observation, one reaches the conclusion, based on interacting facial characteristics and actual experiences, that a certain parent experiences the world primarily through feelings. This person may be asking questions, each time with increased passion; and if you simply try to offer a rational "explanation," you may not succeed. A feeling question needs to be met with empathy. "Why is my child not reading yet?" If such a question arises from a feeling place, it might be met with "This must be a struggle for you and your family." Conversely, a parent may ask, "What is the Waldorf approach to reading?" This may be coming from a thinking point of view and would welcome a clear explanation. Often we don't know the source of a question at first, though human physiology can give us some clues.

In general, I have found it is best to start where a person is in the process and then through conversation, evolve the situation. So a feeling question can be met with empathy and then gradually one can bring in some theory and finish with an action plan (will). A will-initiated question needs to be met concretely; look at the child's work, and then draw out the willing and thinking aspects. Everyone longs for balance these days, and a good parent–teacher conversation can strive for just that (see the following chapter on thinking, feeling, willing).

Parents need to apply their observational skills just as much as teachers. When the teacher asks, "How is Sally doing at home these days?" it could be coming from a feeling, thinking, or willing place, and knowledge of who we are addressing can help. The question from the teacher may be intended simply to establish rapport on a heart level, and a long explanation of household chores may prove mildly irritating. Alternatively, the question may be more about homework assignments that require a more conceptual response. The beauty of the situation is that if our observations are correct, they will work in real life. If they do not, conversation tends to call for a repeat performance; one often needs to try a response from a different angle. All this interaction keeps us flexible, on our toes so to speak. This kind of activity builds mutual engagement and increases the chances of success in relationship building.

Finally, a word about stereotypes: in doing this observational work, one has to avoid shortcuts. It is so easy to stop observing and go to a place of "Dads are more thinking, Moms are more feeling," or "Hispanics are this, Germans are that." This kind of shortcut can lead to serious errors and actual injustice. Each person is unique, and I have found that there are as many variations as there are numbers on this planet. Of course gender and culture influence behavior (more on these topics later), but we always need to stop to really see the person in front of us. Even when we have done considerable observation, life has a way of changing the circumstances, and we must adapt. Thus, a usually cerebral parent may suddenly be devastated by a death in the family. We need to embrace the whole person in all the surrounding circumstances. When we do this, we are modeling something for our children and for humanity as a whole.

4

The Inner Dimensions of Thinking, Feeling, Willing

We each have a dragon within. For some it might be unconscious urges and cravings, for others a smoldering temper. It
is part of the human condition to have to struggle with the dragon
within, and countless myths and legends attest to this battle. Most
notable are the legends of St. Michael and St. George, often depicted
in great works of art. Here one can experience in pictorial form the
higher being taming, sometimes even slaying the dragon.

Children's literature has some wonderful examples that speak
to this imagery, such as the portrayal of Eustice by C. S. Lewis
in the Voyage of the Dawntreader, a spoiled, obnoxious boy who
puts on an arm bracelet only to find himself turned into a dragon.
His internal traits have become externalized. Through much suffering, including social exclusion from his friends, he finds ways to
perform selfless acts of love and eventually Aslan helps him "peel
off" the layers of his dragon nature (painfully) and regain his true
form. We also have Smaug in The Hobbit by J. R. R. Tolkien, as
well as countless other examples, such as Perseus slaying the ven-
omous Medusa. Again and again, the dragon represents the lower
instincts—the disintegration and fragmentation of life.

In Greek mythology, we also see the counterforce in the Sun
god, Apollo. Their revered sun spirit was the harmonizer of what
had become separate through the entrance of selfishness and greed.

"Thou Sun Spirit, Thou hast ensouled Thyself in an etheric spirit form. Thou has brought thinking, feeling, and willing, which might otherwise rage through us in confusion, into order with Thy lyre, sounding upon it harmoniously the tones of the human soul."[1]

Without this deed of Apollo, which can be seen as a pre-earthly deed of Christ, humankind would have been subject to the furies, torn apart by conflicting desires, self-seeking reason, and scornful feelings. Apollo, the Sun Spirit, became the guardian of the wild, stormy passions, the one that brought them back into harmony within the human soul. Apollo was to the Greeks what others represented in the Archangel Michael or St. George in victory over the dragon.

It is still part of the human condition to have feelings, thoughts, and the will to act. We continue to battle for that harmony, that unity of purpose spoken of by the ancient ones. It is not uncommon for a person to feel one way and yet say something else, or leave a meeting with a verbal agreement only to act differently afterward. At times, our thinking, feeling, and willing still struggle against fragmentation and disintegration.

This inner battle affects the parent–teacher relationship. Sometimes we truly mean well but cannot follow through. Alternatively, we may be overheard saying something that we regret afterward. Our intentions are not always aligned with our outer words and actions. Time and again we need to apologize or retrace our steps to bring about healing.

I have found that when parents and teachers can gather to do artistic work, much harmonizing occurs. For example, if a teacher is the recipient of many theoretical, head oriented questions in a class night, she might suggest a "musical stretch" in which everyone gets out of their chairs and does an interactive, joyful musical game. After just a few minutes, the parents will sit down again with smiles, quips, and jovial remarks that come from a feeling place.

---

1   Steiner, *Four Sacrifices of Christ*, 11.

Balance has returned in an effortless way. It matters not so much what art form one selects (although they do have difference effects) but more important is including in a class evening some singing, drama, painting, or drawing. We find each other in our humanity when we do art together, and we re-harmonize within. Then parents and teachers can sit down and discuss the matters at hand out of a place of inner wholeness.

Integrate through the arts.

5

Barriers

As I write this section, I have cotton in my left ear due to an ear infection. This has temporarily affected my hearing. Life is full of little challenges. Thank goodness many of them are temporary. But we need to deal with them, or else the occasional ear infection could become something much worse, especially for a person who loves music.

Likewise, there are barriers to parent participation in school life. Here are a few as described by Maryln Appelbaum in her book *How to Handle Hard-to-Handle Parents*:

LANGUAGE BARRIERS. These are more common currently in many schools, as we have many parents who have limited English, so when they come to school they can feel out of place and embarrassed. These folks may stop going to school events altogether and just rely on their child to tell them what is happening.

SINGLE-PARENT BARRIERS. According to some studies, more than 30% of all children in the United States live in single-parent homes.[1] In the traditional nuclear family there is often a division of responsibilities but, in the single-parent home, everything falls to one person. In addition to a full day of work, sometimes even holding down multiple jobs and facing a daily commute, the single parent does all the cooking, cleaning, packing of lunches, and so on, and by the time the evening of the class night arrives, she or he can

---

1   Appelbaum, *Hard to Handle Parents*, 7.

be extremely tired. It is not that she does not want to go to school, or that she does not love her children, it is just that most of the time she is in survival mode.

NEGATIVE-EXPERIENCE BARRIERS. For some parents, going into a school building reminds them of their own negative experiences as a child. Some of these experiences may have been forgotten for years, but then well up with great feeling when back in a classroom sitting in a child-size chair. My father-in-law was a boy who always seemed to get on the wrong side of teachers—his stories could be both shocking and amusing. But it takes many years to get perspective on these things, and for some young parents the memories remain compelling.

DIVERSITY BARRIERS. Some parents may not come to school because they are in a minority and cannot be sure if they will be valued or respected. Unfortunately, as with the other barriers mentioned, this may be true in some schools. This is not just a matter of language, but extends into issues such as clothing, economic status and those with physical or mental handicaps. Some may be veterans who have both visible and not so visible scars from their service to our country.

In all these instances, schools and teachers in particular need to adopt strategies to reach all their parents. In speaking with those who have been most successful at this, a multimodal approach seems to be the way to go. For some parents it is more frequent emails, others need a note home, others prefer a phone call. I have had cases of a parent–teacher dialogue book serving the purpose of informal back and forth. Schools also need access to translators, and of course, are federally mandated to be accessible. Arranging babysitting for early evening class nights can help, as planning the all-American potluck followed by childcare and class night. Above all, when in doubt, one can ask: how can I help? What works for you? Once one comes into conversation, solutions often rise up, even from the children of the parents in question. Children, at least those in the younger years, want their parents involved, and they often come up with the most ingenious solutions when we ask for help. Parents will often make good suggestions as to how to remove obstacles to participation. And there are professionals in most communities who can give advice on group dynamics and facilitation. But we need to recognize that barriers exist and sincerely seek ways to remove hindrances to parent–teacher collaboration.

6

Relationships and Martin Buber

*S*ome years ago I was talking with an experienced teacher who said, "At my last school I learned how to deal with parents. I no longer let them push me around. One has to be firm and let them know who is in charge." Of course one can see where this teacher is coming from, and yes, the teacher is "in charge" in the classroom. But the whole encounter left me feeling a bit like she had been talking about stinging nettles—objects—not people. Likewise, I have at times heard parents refer to a particular teacher as "arrogant" or "uptight," characteristics that may have had some basis in reality, but again, left me feeling as if people were being degraded.

Turning a person into an "it" instead of valuing the inherent spirit in each reminded me of a wise philosopher I read in graduate school many years ago who addressed these kinds of issues. Thus recently I found reason to return to the great Jewish writer, Martin Buber, who describes the difference between an "I–It" relationship and an "I–Thou" relationship:

The life of human beings is not passed in the sphere of transitive verbs alone. It does not exist in virtue of activities alone, which have some thing for their object.

I perceive something. I am sensible of something. I imagine something. I will something. I feel something. I think something. The life of human beings does not consist of all this and the like alone.

This and the like together establish the realm of It.

But the realm of Thou has a different basis. When Thou *is spoken, the speaker has no thing for his object; where there is a thing, there is also another thing. Every It is bounded by others; It exists only by being bounded by others. But when* Thou *is spoken, there is no thing; Thou has no bounds. When* Thou *is spoken, the speaker has no thing; one has indeed nothing but takes a stand in relation.*[1]

So many of our social issues today are connected to this dynamic: treating people as an "it" vs. living in Thou*, "which has no bounds." Rather than diminishing and circumscribing with "it," the speaker can risk standing in transition (nothing) and come to a place of "relation," which is alive and filled with spirit.*

The spheres in which the world of relations arises are three. First, our life with nature. There the relation sways in gloom, beneath the level of speech. Creatures live and move over against us, but cannot come to us, and when we address them as Thou, our words cling to the threshold of speech. Second, our life with other human beings. There, the relationship is open and in the form of speech. We can give and accept the Thou. Third, our life with spiritual beings. There the relation is clouded, yet it discloses itself; it does not use speech, yet begets it. We perceive no Thou, but we nonetheless feel we are addressed, and we answer—forming, thinking, acting. We speak the primary word with our being, though we cannot utter Thou *with our lips.*[2] *Or to put it even more succinctly:*

The world of It is set in the context of space and time.
The world of Thou is not set in the context of either of these.
The particular Thou, after the relational event has run its course,
    is bound to become an It.
The particular It, by entering the relational event, may become
    a Thou.[3]

---

1   Buber, *I and Thou*, 4.

2   Ibid., 6.

3   Ibid., 33.

Both the It *and the* Thou *are important for our lives: "And in all the seriousness of truth, hear this: without It man cannot live. But he who lives with It alone is not a man."*[4]

So the question becomes, in which areas of life do we use It and when and how can we work out of Thou? Buber would say that the It realm of life has to do with experiencing, using, sustaining life, and having the equipment we need to function. It is all about utilization, technology. However at a certain point all this can become an obstacle to further growth. As human beings we need the Thou, for this aspect of life has to do directly with the spirit:

> *Spirit in its human manifestation is a response of man to his Thou. Man speaks with many tongues, tongues of language, of art, of action; but the spirit is one, the response to the Thou which appears and addresses him out of the mystery. Spirit is the word. And just as talk in a language may well first take the form of words in the brain of the man, and then sound in his throat, and yet both are merely refractions of the true event, for in actuality speech does not abide in man, but man takes his stand in speech and talks from there; so with every word and every spirit. Spirit is not in the I, but between I and Thou. It is not like the blood that circulates in you, but like the air in which you breathe. Man lives in the spirit, if he is able to respond to his Thou. He is able to, if he enters into relation with his whole being. Only in virtue of his power to enter into relation is he able to live in the spirit.*
>
> *But the destiny of the relational event is here set forth in the most powerful way. The stronger the response the more strongly does it bind up the Thou and banish it to be an object. Only silence before the Thou—silence of all tongues, silent patience in the undivided word that precedes the formed and vocal response—leaves the Thou free, and permits man to take his stand with it in the reserve where the spirit is not manifest, but is.*[5]

---

4   Ibid., 34.

5   Ibid., 39.

One can understand the Quaker "meeting" with these eloquent words: the silence of all tongues, the "silent patience in the undivided word that precedes the formed and vocal response." How can we practice this in the parent–teacher relationship, indeed in all relationships?

In the true sense in which Buber intended, I–Thou is a purely spiritual state, so any examples run the risk of defaming the great man. However, we are all "on the way" and in that spirit, one can look for instances in which we can begin to move from a simple I–It world to one in which things are lifted to I–Thou. So for the sake of illustration, one can take a typical nonprofit and look at how it might move from one state of existence to another:

I–IT	I–THOU
Board meetings/ the organization is present	The mission lives in member conversation wherever it takes place
Members pay set dues	Members willingly participate in financial support
The headquarters are the organization	The organization lives in member activities anywhere
The annual report	Member interactions on the web site

This list could continue, but the point is that in an age in which formal relationships have broken down and old assumptions are questioned, moving from a basis of I–It to I–Thou in a nonprofit could breathe new life into the organization. We all have experienced buildings that take on the feeling of a mausoleum—cold, uninhabited, a receptionist who seems surprised someone walked in. We know what it is like to enter a room filled with people in conversation. We need to move our organizations from an identity that rests on place and things (It) toward activity centers that find their life through human interaction (Thou). Many of our existential challenges would be meet if we could reestablish our nonprofit organizations based on the purely human encounter.

7

Hard-to-Handle Parents

Maryln Appelbaum begins, in her book *Hard to Handle Parents*, with six "Nevers" for the teacher and then suggests some very practical strategies for success:

Never argue.
Never get defensive.
Never raise your voice.
Never say or do anything for which you have to make amends.
Never take it personally.
Never lose your cool.[1]

Of course one could add to this list—never make a mistake. In my experience, all of the above is easier said than done. One way to summarize would be to say: stay professional, for you are always "the teacher" even in informal situations. And when your buttons are getting pushed, you can at least step aside, ask for a conference a few days later, or do something to avoid the worst manifestations of the above list. Time away often is the best help, but there are also many other strategies we can use:

The Sandwich Technique. Let's say a parent requests that her son take time off from doing homework and the teacher has already said "No" to other requests and wants to use a softer approach without giving ground. So here is the sandwich:

Bread: It is great that you are so concerned about your son.

---

1 Appelbaum, *Hard to Handle Parents*, 29.

The Ingredient: It will not work for him to take time off and not do any homework. He would fall behind the other students.

Bread: Thank you so much for your concern. We both want him to succeed.[2]

The Repetition Response. Sometimes a teacher simply has to say the same thing time and again. For example, we can repeatedly emphasize that homework is not just about "getting it done," but also about building good work habits.

Set a time to meet. This gives both of you a space in which to prepare and come with a plan. Offer choices about when to meet and stay positive. For example, one might use the phrase, "When we next meet, let's look at other options for helping John succeed."

Once you have found a comfortable place to meet, open the meeting by setting a mutually agreed-upon goal. Where do you want to be at the end of the conversation? This goal setting brings out agreement early on in the process, even if it is a general one such as "We both want Saun to find more friends."

Be sure to listen. This sounds obvious, but there are some particular ways in which your listening can be communicated, such as taking notes, not interrupting, nodding your head and summarizing at the end.

It really helps to talk about possible solutions, to brainstorm various ways to achieve your agreed upon goal. Even if some of the choices are not what you would feel comfortable with, make sure you both explore them, as it draws everyone into the problem solving process. You can always refine and edit later.

Finalize a plan of action. This might involve several steps and should be something that is doable.

Agree to check in again in a few days to follow up and evaluate. Make sure you have each other's correct contact information.

---

2   Ibid., 36.

*Try to end in a pleasant way, with expressions of appreciation
and something positive about the meeting, the class, or the student.*[3]

This may all seem self-evident, but when things get difficult one
needs more form/structure. A 2005 *Time* magazine article cited
three-quarters of teachers saying that parents treat them as adver-
saries.[4] Some parents seem to approach teachers in general with a
bad, and one needs tools in the toolbox for these situations.

One such tool is humor. I am not suggesting that teachers or
parents become comedians, but as I have grown older, I have found
that humor can help us navigate through some of the most challenging human situations. My children say that I tell bad jokes, so I tend
to avoid formal joke telling (at least in their presence). But there are
many other ways to bring in humor. One of the most effective is
anything that shows one can laugh at oneself. We all find ourselves
in ridiculous situations from time to time, and telling such a story
can lighten up the entire exchange. Things happen in life, and part
of our navigation through the unexpected involves being able to
look at events at times as if they were happening to someone else.
We are more comical than we think, sometimes in absurd ways. So,
here is an instance that my youngest son has asked me to tell again
and again when we have house guests:

Some time ago, I went to Agway to buy some birdseed for my
wife—well, not really for her but for the outdoor birds she loves.
I found a fifty-pound block of suet with a handle that said, "Lift
here." I dutifully did that, carried it through the store and as I lifted
it up onto the counter to pay, it broke, rotated and a corner fell on
my big toe. I knew right away that the damage was serious, went
home and put ice on it and planned to keep it elevated for the rest
of the day.

This went well (it is not often one can have some enforced idle-
ness in a La-Z-Boy chair). In fact, I sort of forgot about the toe, so
when our daughter Louisa came in to say she had missed her bus

---

3   Ibid., paraphrased, 46.

4   Ibid., 35.

back to college, I volunteered to drive her—a three hour trip each way. To make a long story short, I barely made it. We carried her stuff up three flights of stairs and I started home again, as the toe was now swelling within my shoe. On the way back, it began to hurt so badly I had to pull off the road and check into a motel. I peeled off the sock and found a large, purple mass where my toe used to be. I called my wife to tell her I was not coming home, and while on the phone, hobbling around the hotel room looking for ice, I passed out. I came to a few minutes later on the rug, and was shocked to see lacerations all over my face where I had hit the rug. I somehow managed to dress and get myself into the emergency room, where they drilled into the nail to relieve the pressure and bandaged me up.

For the next two days I hobbled around with a large clubfoot and lacerations all over my face. When I told my wife I had to go to Portland for a meeting, she was aghast. She thought it was Portland, Maine, and protested vigorously when she learned it was Portland, Oregon. Nevertheless I got myself to Logan, hobbled onto the plane in my freshly dry-cleaned business clothes and sat down for what I hoped would be a five-hour nap. As they were deicing the plane, a teenage boy behind me suddenly got sick, and a wall of vomit cascaded over the back of my seat and over my head just as I had dozed off. So there I was, hobbling down the isle, covered in vomit, hoping I could remove some of the damage in the tiny restroom. The damage to the seats was so serious they brought the plane back to the gate, two men in white decontamination suits came aboard, and the boy and his mother were asked to leave the plane. She handed me $10 for dry cleaning as she left!

When we were finally at 30,000 feet a flight attendant came to me and said, "You handled that so well, we would like to give you some extra FF miles... but there is no category in our system for what you went through. Let's see... I will award you 5,000 miles for 'medical assistance.'" I arrived in Portland safely, but when my host picked me up and we were sitting in the car, my first question was,

"Do you smell anything?" Needless to say, we made a detour to my hotel before I walked into my first meeting.

If I am honest with myself, I think the reason Ionas asks me to tell that story so often is that he likes to imagine his father in a ridiculous situation, and I suspect many of us take ourselves too seriously. But in terms of the story itself, it reveals the lengths to which a parent will go for a daughter, the foolishness of not listening to one's partner and cancelling a trip and how life seems to cut us all back down to size once in a while. If we can look at ourselves and events with a humor-filled attitude, we are more likely to connect with others who have had unusual experiences. This commonality of experience and knowing others who can laugh at themselves can lead to human bonds that serve in countless ways in the future. This bond is a substance as real as food and drink; only we seldom give it the same level of attention. Laugh and we shall heal.

8

The Third Space

*I*n 1913, Rudolf Steiner began to build a home for the
*Anthroposophical Society on a hill in northeastern Switzerland,
within view of both France and Germany. His choice, given the
advent of World War I, and then many years later, World War II,
was particularly appropriate, and people from many nationalities
were able to gather in neutral Switzerland to join in the construction. The result of many years work was a building called the first
Goetheanum (see photo).*

*Although very much one organic whole, the architecture of the
building consisted of two intersecting domes, one larger than the
other. Both were covered with Norwegian slate that could reflect
the changing light and shadows from the sky. The rest of the structure was made of wood, with the exception of the concrete base.
The larger dome housed the auditorium and faced west, while the
smaller dome, enclosing the stage, faced east. (See diagram.)*

*Henry Barnes, in "The Third Space," picks up the narrative
with the following words:*

> *If each dome stood alone, its ground plan would be a per-
> fect circle. Because they intersect, both the circle formed by
> the outer walls that support the domes, and the inner circle
> formed by the columns supporting the interior ceilings, form
> an architectural space that is common to both spheres. This
> "third" space, however, not only unites but also separates.*

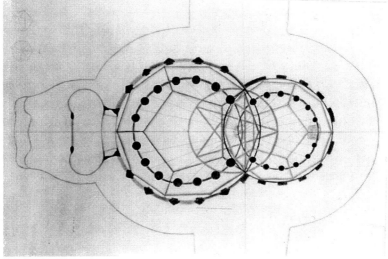

*The first Goetheanum and general floor plan
showing larger and smaller domes*

*In this sense it is a "threshold" that can become a key to an
understanding of the entire structure.*[1]

*There is an aspect of faculty/staff work that is a self-enclosed
circle: pedagogical decisions, school policies, and curriculum*

---

1   Barnes, in "The Third Space," 11.

*rightfully belong in the purview of those who are trained profes-
sionals in these areas. It would be wrong to have parents entangled
in these matters, just as when I go to a dentist I rely on his or her
professional expertise. Likewise, the circle of parents in a school
can be seen as a second circle—one that has to do with child-rear-
ing and matters of home life, and so on, which should be distinct
from the school. Yet as we know so well, the two circles overlap in
many areas: issues such as homework, the amount of sleep a child
is getting at night, and attendance are mutual concern. Here we
have the "third space" in which the work of parents and teachers
overlaps. This third space is the relationship zone.*

Henry Barnes continues his description:

> *The two spheres, the sphere of the seven and that of the
> twelve, are in themselves polarities—one might say almost
> irreconcilable polarities. Every human being is welcome to
> enter the sphere of the seven, the auditorium, if he or she
> wants to hear or see what goes on there. Christian or Jew,
> Buddhist or Mohammedan, agnostic or atheist, are equally
> welcome. They have only to take the initiative to come, to
> observe, and, if they so wish, to participate and understand.
> Each has a right to be there and to accept or reject what goes
> on. Here, each is equal.*[2]

*Here we have the sphere of public education, the right of every
child to schooling, as envisioned by Horace Mann, John Dewy and
countless others. Even in an independent school, there is a sphere of
equal rights, in that each parent, once their child is enrolled, has a
right to a place in that auditorium, has the right to participate without discrimination. The parent body in many respects represents
the res-publica, the community. A healthy school needs the breadth
and input that comes from an engaged public.*

*The smaller, interior space, however, is grounded in the twelve.
This space speaks of objective, cosmic realities. Here, Hierarchy is
at home. It is meaningless to vote whether four times four is twelve*

---

2   Ibid., 12.

or sixteen, or twenty. In this sphere, hierarchy is neither arbitrary nor static, but exists in archetypal lawfulness.[3]

So this second dome is the home of the faculty/staff/administration. These are people who, we hope, did not just wander in, but were hired based upon their expertise. It is a sphere of hierarchy: not everyone can teach French, or manage the finances of the school. Chaos would result if these positions were subject to a vote as in the larger dome. As stated there is a strict lawfulness in how faculty and staff work, as one cannot just make up an answer to four times four. There is a need for strong, internal accountability, as in peer evaluation and professional standards.

Yet there are inherent dangers to both spheres:

> *Each sphere has its rightful place and function, yet in each a potential tyranny is hidden. One might say of the sphere of the twelve that it hides a potential "theocratic tyranny," a tyranny of truth that becomes dogma. But the sphere of the seven also hides a potential tyranny: the "democratic," for which every truth is relative, every insight personal and subjective. In a social organism, how can these potential tyrannies be reconciled? Can they come together in any kind of functioning whole? This is, I believe, where the "third space" emerges as a saving grace.*[4]

This third space is where the speaker might stand where the two circles intersect, a person who may have achieved significant learning, but has to also let it die, to let go so as to leave the audience in the larger hall free. Out of letting go, the speaker then works with the audience to see what comes to life, just as a dramatic performer works with the audience in a living way. And members of the audience have to likewise "let go" of preconceived notions and attitudes so as to fully experience what is shared. This mutual act of taking in and letting go in both spheres is a rhythmic process. It

---

3   Ibid.

4   Ibid.

represents the "mood of the threshold" that lifts each one beyond their normal "selves."

So for both a teacher and a parent, it is possible to enter this third space in which more is created than the sum of the two. In the human encounter one can have a threshold experience in which new insight is born, insight that is the result of the breadth brought forward by the parent and the depth of a teacher's pedagogical understanding. The third space is often found in-between, the moments between sentences, between meetings, between coming and going. So if we can pause sometimes in a dialogue, or ask for a followup meeting, a night to ponder, then we are opening a third space for spiritual insight to enter. The in-between or third space is then an opportunity for grace, and the spiritual worlds often respond with a gift of insight. The work of parents and teachers can then be seen as an earthly sacrament, a blessing on the school and all the children within.

9

Hammershus

In August 2013, Ionas, Karine and I returned to her island of birth in the Baltic Sea. At the northern tip of Bornholm we tramped up the hill to visit the old medieval castle called Hammershus. Built in 1200 and in use for about 500 years, all that remains today are parts of the walls and interior buildings. Standing at the periphery one can look out at the Baltic Sea and imagine incoming vessels and the hustle and bustle of medieval castle life.

Later that day we went out in a small boat and explored the grottos along that same coastline. In one instance we even went inside a long, narrow cave, a kind of watery tunnel into the mountain— legend has it that once they lost a goose in there and days later it came out the other side of the island! When back out at sea again, I looked up at Hammershus, this time from the vantage point of the ocean. With those sheer cliffs it would not have been easy to assail that fortress. There are times when a school can resemble aspects of a medieval castle:

For those living in the surrounding countryside, you are either In or Out.

The portcullis seems to open more readily for some than for others.

For those with an errand (or question) one often has to wait a while for the messenger (we now call them assistants) to return with word from on high.

There is a hierarchy within the castle that is not always visible or comprehensible.

There are castle "intrigues" that baffle and confound those outside the inner circle.

When attacked, or even if there is a perceived attack, the gates close.

Emissaries often speak in a medieval tongue that is hard to understand.

Those in the countryside are expected to pay regular tithes and offer volunteer labor for the upkeep of the castle. In the case of Hammershus, it was cords of wood until after years the island was deforested.

Wandering minstrels are favored; we now call them consultants.

Edicts are issued without explanation (today we call them decisions), and if one asks for clarifications or a rationale one can be seen as "unsupportive."

There are lords and ladies, and some play the part well and others just want control.

Teachers and administrators need to beware of the castle phenomena. A school can be a formidable place just in terms of structure and internal navigation. But it is inherent in the nature of organizations that over time they take on more form and structure, and sometimes without even intending to, an organization can become calcified. Teachers can become unapproachable, and process can morph into procedure. Over time there is more and more emphasis on filling out the right forms and talking to people up the chain of command rather than simply talking. Committees can obscure individual responsibility, and personal agendas can hide behind committee structures. "The staffing committee has decided..." may be the official communication but in fact everyone knows that it was Mrs. S who decided once again who would be hired, fired or marginalized.

This phenomenon presents a huge challenge for parents, especially those who have workplace skills that allow them to see through

*Hammershus, northern Europe's largest medieval fortification,
on the northern tip of the Danish island Bornholm, in the Baltic Sea*

the façade. Often it is a parent who will call the question, serve as the canary in the coal mine. But do we have the ears to hear? I have found that many teachers adopt a defensive posture in regard to parents. They seem to worry that any remark will be a criticism, and they shut down to real input. Parents often get defensive when their child's behaviors are discussed, immediately assuming that it is a reflection on their parenting skills. When both parties get defensive, it can become a game of ice hockey with the child as the puck being batted back and forth. Many parent–teacher interactions can then boil down to posturing:

The teacher wants to appear to know the answer to any question and stay in control of the dialogue.

The parent plays up to the teacher with all sorts of volunteerism and useful help, hoping that their family will look good in the eyes of the teacher and the school.

But when there is too much posturing, the one who loses out is the child. Direct, honest dialogue, give and take, giving and receiving feedback is necessary if parents and teachers are to get to the heart of an issue.

How can a faculty and staff avoid "group think" and open their hearts and minds to information that may challenge some of their deepest assumptions? How can parents raise issues in a non-threatening way? And when some on the faculty and staff hear these issues and advance them in a faculty meeting, will their colleagues give them a chance to explain?

Especially in Waldorf schools where there is a deep-seated philosophical basis for consensus decision-making and high ideals for the education, it is essential that teachers and parents walk the talk.

How to keep an organization healthy and vibrant is the main focus of my book *Organizational Integrity*, so I will not go into further detail here. But both parents and teachers should keep in mind the castle metaphor and guard against the construction of unintended walls.

10

At the Foundation

*W*hen the Goetheanum burned to the ground in the tragic fire
of New Years Eve, 1922/23, something entirely new had to
come into being. Thus, although Rudolf Steiner designed and began
to build a new Goetheanum (see picture), he put the greatest emphasis on the needed change and laid the Foundation Stone Meditation
in the hearts and minds of members of the Anthroposophical
Society. The words he spoke were forged by Steiner's pleading with
the spiritual worlds, and we can gratefully regard the Foundation
Stone Meditation as a doorway that has been given to us so that
we can actively take up its spiritual substance. To this day, the
Foundation Stone verses are spoken in languages all over the world
as a call for the dawn of a new form of consciousness.

Although each of the first three panels (or verses) of the Foundation
Stone Meditation begins in the same way, "Human Soul," they are
indeed three very different expressions of human nature. Having
lived with the words for many years, I have found that the possibilities for understanding are inexhaustible. As I began to prepare for
this book on parent–teacher relations, I found that the three panels
spoke eloquently to the three dimensions of the work of a school:
the parent, teacher, and child.

The second Goetheanum

We may work with the complete Foundation Stone Meditation for an extended time to take advantage of what follows. With all humility, I will try to draw forth several aspects that pertain to the theme of this book.

I.   The role of the parent as seen
     through the lens of the first panel

> *Human Soul!*
> *You live within the limbs*
> *Which bear you through the world of space*
> *Into the spirits' ocean-being:*
> *Practice spirit recalling*
> *In depths of soul,*
> *Where in the wielding*
> *World-Creator-Being*
> *Your own I*
> *Comes into being*

In the I of God;
And you will truly live
In human world-all-being.
For the Father-Spirit of the heights holds sway
In depths of worlds begetting life.
Spirits of Strength:
Let ring forth from the heights
What in the depths is echoed,
Speaking:
Out of the Godhead we are born.

In the first panel, we have many key words that speak to the initiation path we commonly call parenting.

Spirit-recalling: Where do I come from? What is my heritage and the story of my family? Where have I been in this life and before? Do I remember you?

You will truly live: Begetting life—as parents, we have brought a new life into the world, and we know firsthand something of the mystery of birth.

For the Father-Spirit of the heights holds sway: Many cultures and traditions speak of the Father or Mother principles, the ground of existence, the foundation of all being. Old sayings refer to Mother Earth and Father Sun. Again, this is the basis of life on Earth.

Out of the Godhead we are born: A singular, strong origin for all who inhabit this world.

These phrases all have singular, primal qualities that live at first in the depths of the unconscious. Parenting comes from this place of quiet strength. Like a Titan of the ancient Greeks, a parent can move great obstacles in protection of one's offspring. The parent represents the Ur-beings, the old wisdom of heritage and tradition.

II. *The role of the teacher as seen through the lens of the second panel*

> *Human soul!*
> *You live within the beat of heart and lung*
> *Which leads you through the rhythms of time*
> *Into the feeling of your own soul-being:*
> *Practice spirit-sensing*
> *In balance of the soul,*
> *Where the surging deeds*
> *Of World-evolving*
> *Unite your own I*
> *With the I of the World;*
> *And you will truly feel*
> *In human soul's creating.*
> *For the Christ-will encircling us holds sway,*
> *In world rhythms, bestowing grace upon souls.*
> *Spirits of Light:*
> *Let from the east be enkindled*
> *What through the west takes on form,*
> *Speaking:*
> *In Christ death becomes life.*

In the second panel, we have many key words that speak to the initiative path we commonly call teaching.

Within the beat of heart and lung: This leads us through the rhythms of time; the path of the teacher, especially in a Waldorf school, is one of rhythm. At the very beginning of his first course for teachers, Rudolf Steiner spoke of the importance of breathing. In Waldorf education, rhythm replaces strength.

Practice spirit sensing: This is what a good teacher does all day! Who is this child before me? What are the child's needs? What is this class asking of me today? True teachers live in the present, constantly sensing and experiencing what is happening in the Now.

In Christ, death becomes life: Knowledge, especially as we have it all around us conventionally, is often about dead things—dead facts, dead books, and dead science. The art of teaching is to take what is dead and breathe life into it, so that children can experience it with their living souls. So rather than facts about Abraham Lincoln, the teacher strives to enact scenes from his life, his stories, his mannerisms, just as the actor Daniel Day Lewis did in the recent film Lincoln. The teacher is the bringer of life.

III. *In service of the Child as seen through the lens of the third panel*

> *Human Soul!*
> *You live within the resting head*
> *Which from the grounds of eternity*
> *Unlocks for you world-thoughts:*
> *Practice spirit-beholding*
> *In stillness of thought,*
> *Where the gods' eternal aims*
> *Bestow the light of cosmic being*
> *On your own I*
> *For free and active willing.*
> *And you will truly think*
> *In human spirit depths.*
> *For the Spirit's world-thoughts hold sway*
> *In cosmic being, imploring light.*
> *Spirits of Soul:*
> *Let from the depths be entreated*
> *What in the heights be heard,*
> *Speaking:*
> *In the spirit's cosmic thoughts, the soul awakens.*

In the third panel, we have aspects of the child and student in our care.

Which from the grounds of eternity: Children are the most recent arrivals from the spiritual worlds and they often remind us of their eternal origin.

Spirits of Soul: They live in the soul realm and real teaching brings them content to nourish the soul life.

In the spirit's cosmic thoughts, the soul awakens: All Waldorf education is an awakening of soul capacities. We begin with willing, then educate the feeling, and then stand back in awe as thoughts awaken in the students.

There are of course many other ways to work with the Foundation Stone Meditation, but for the purposes of the parent, teacher, child, I wanted to indicate that there are seeds here that could nourish our inner connection to the threefold aspect of our work in schools.

We are incomplete without all three panels, without the limbs, the heart, the head, or without the encircling embrace of parents, teachers, and children. As three, we are whole, and can move into the fourth panel, the new beginning. But this is a subject for another chapter.

Communication

One might say that communication is the "heart" of all par-ent–teacher relations. When it goes well, life can be smooth sailing, and occasional squalls are dealt with promptly. When communication is not flowing, almost nothing else works. Just as with the human heart, communication is the crossroads, the great meeting place for much of what happens among adults in and around a school.

I would like to begin with Marshall Rosenberg and his valuable work on nonviolent communication. His efforts have been taken up by John Cunningham and others who have found both philosophical and practical perspectives for this theme. They differentiate between "onlooker consciousness and participatory consciousness":

ONLOOKER CONSCIOUSNESS: "This language is from the head. It is a way of mentally classifying people into varying shades of good and bad, right and wrong. Ultimately, it provokes defensiveness, resistance, and counterattack. It is a language of demands."[1] Here are some of the manifestations of onlooker consciousness:

JUDGING: moralistic judgments, good/bad/ and right/wrong, either/or, binary thinking.

BLAMING: faultfinding, deviance detecting.

---

1   Cunningham, *Compassionate Communication*, p. 6.

LABELING: classifying and categorizing, sexist, racist and other stereotypes, you to it.

OBEYING: denying choice, denying responsibility, conditioned to authority.

DESERVE: punishment and reward, behavior modification, dominator mentalities.

COMPARING: measuring, testing, grading, and competing for winners and losers.

BEING RIGHT: convincing and persuading, debating and arguing, "enlightening" others.

ASSUMING: interpretations, analysis and diagnoses, jumping to conclusions.[2]

So much in today's world has brought us to this place of observer consciousness. We look at others as if from a distance and see them as objects (*I–it relationships*). Our language, as seen in the above descriptors, becomes more and more negative. In the process, our humanity is degraded and we find it harder and harder to get along. Fortunately, Rosenberg has worked on a methodology to reclaim understanding and partnership through what he calls *Participatory Consciousness:*

OBSERVATIONS—here one strives to state what it is without any spin. One tries to stay factual, observation bound. This is what a video camera might record. One looks for common ground and welcomes clarifications from others.

Feelings—the task here is to differentiate feelings from thoughts, for they give us information while thoughts tend to interpret. One strives to share feelings as in "I feel that…I feel that…so others can be brought into your experiences.

NEEDS—Here again, one tries to differentiate between needs, which are universal; everyone has them, and strategies,

---

2   Cunningham, *Compassionate Communication*, 6.

which tend to be more personal and specific. When we share our needs our language reveals our human becoming and the basis for our feelings. Expressing our needs connects us to our shared humanity and fosters compassionate connection.

REQUESTS—these are very different from demands, as they have no conditions, while demands do. When making a request, it is best to be positive, concrete. Ask for things that are doable in the present or near future. Both parties should strive to meet the other person's requests, and clarify what has been heard.[3]

Rosenberg and Cunningham have developed workshops and exercises that can help move people from the onlooker consciousness to that of participatory consciousness. Dieter Brüll in *The Mysteries of Social Encounters* states, "The social aspect of the spiritual life demands that I open myself to the other, invite him to express himself in me. In this way I am able to experience his questions of inner development as my own."[4] So how can observations, feelings, needs, and requests work in a real-life parent–teacher situation? Here is an example provided by John:

Parent says to the teacher: "The class is out of control and my daughter is miserable" (a phrase that is loaded with onlooker consciousness). Or the parent could rephrase:

When I see how unhappy my daughter is when she comes home and tells me about some things that happen at school.... (Observations)

I'm feeling heartbroken and alarmed... (Feelings)

Because I need clarity about what's going on for my daughter. I need to know that she is safe and supported at school. (Needs for clarity)

---

3   Cunningham, 7.
4   Cunningham, 7.

Would you be willing to share with me what you see happening and the steps you're taking to foster harmony among the children? (Requests).[5]

Or an example from the teacher side: "It seems Jason is spending way too much time watching screens and he can't focus at all in class." Or the rephrase: When I see how Jason struggles to stay focused on his schoolwork and he tells me he spends a lot of time at home watching TV or on the computer, and I reflect on what I've read about sensory-integration and child development.... (Observations)

I feel concerned and helpless... (Feelings)

Because I need support for my efforts to protect this process of human development that happens in children. (Needs)

Would you be willing to tell me what you're hearing me say? (Request).[6]

This last request is very interesting. On one level it might appear at first as condescending, after all one has to assume the parent has two ears. Yet in real life, what is said and what is heard are often two different things. Checking for understanding, especially around controversial topics such as media, is a good technique for communicating. Sometimes the response will be emotional or tangential, but then one has a chance to amend and clarify right in the moment. Catching things "in the moment" can be crucial before incorrect stories are told to partners and out in the parking lot. Error can occur both from the "teller" as well as the "listener," and both have a responsibility to clarity and to check for understanding. As I often say, one can disagree, but at least be sure you have an accurate picture of what it is!

Receiving an accurate picture means that one has done everything possible to remove roadblocks to good listening. Most of these hindrances are internal; we have certain habitual ways of listening that can get in the way of really receiving what is said. For example, when some people listen, they are inwardly immediately comparing

---

5   Cunningham, Compassionate Communication, p. 12.

6   Ibid., p. 13.

what is said to other instances, or they begin to rehearse an answer before the speaker is finished. Still others go into a judgmental mode, or they begin preparing advice. Others try to divert the speaker with anecdotes, or placate with words such as "you are right...yes I see..." even before the sharing is over. Parents and teachers alike need to examine their listening habits and try to open clear pathways to complete listening. (For a more complete description see "Roadblocks to Listening" in the appendices.)

With six children, my wife and I have had ample opportunity to practice communication skills, both on the home front and with teachers at schools. For the most part, communication pathways have been smooth and easy. Teachers appreciate hearing from parents, and we have felt welcome. Some encourage notes, others emails, and recently we have had the pleasure of a teacher who, when he sees us pass by his room, always says, "Come on in!"

The doorway of a classroom is like an invisible membrane separating the home/parent world and the hub of activity we know as "school" (see the chapter, "The Door"). The way a teacher handles that crossing can indicate many other aspects of communication. Some teachers stand at the door as guardians, others center their focus on the task at hand. If one has to collect an overdue library book that is in your child's desk, does the teacher ask you to stay at the door while she gets it, or are you encouraged to go in yourself? There is no wrong or right way to handle these things, but I have learned to watch the doorway as symbolic of parent–teacher relations.

We had one teacher who tried a variety of techniques at communication. One year she announced that she would not take calls at home and would like parents to send in notes, which should be placed in a box outside the door. Next year the request was for parents to call the school for an appointment, which often meant that we were lost in the maze of voicemails and/or staffing of the front desk. The following year we were all given communication folders, which were supposed to go to and from school each day.

However, as any experienced person would have known, the vast majority of parents did not have anything to communicate many days of the week, so 24 folders went to and from home every day for a year, usually empty. They were eventually beaten up and looked shabby, and children would occasionally be reprimanded for forgetting them. All these attempts within three years! In the end, it all amounted to teacher insecurity over communication, and no "tool" could compensate for that basic human condition.

From a teacher's perspective, I have found that communication is intimately tied up with the person we are working with. I try to calibrate my style based upon the "who" rather than resort to something formulaic. Just as every child is a unique being, so it is with parents. At least half of my interest in communication has to do with getting to know with whom I am working. The other half, of course, is the content of the communication. Above all, however, the most important thing in my view is that we have a welcoming attitude toward parents. In other words, extend a sincere interest in parents' lives, careers, and families; this forms the foundation of a successful partnership.

At an early class night I facilitated a conversation about "what works for you and what works for me" in terms of communication. Parents have a variety of needs, and in some cases I had to say that it would be hard to meet certain ones. Yet for the most part, they are reasonable. On my part, I asked for phone calls and emails before 8:00 p.m. so I could focus on preparation of the lessons after that time. Emergency calls were okay any time, but routine things, such as "Jen has a dentist appointment today" could be handled with a note. I scheduled regular parent–teacher conferences, but kept two or three periods open each week for unscheduled conversations. In short, I tried a multimodal approach, and soon found that different methods worked best for different parents, and it was not that hard to adjust. A teacher's job is to serve.

Finally, a word about confidence and trust: If one devotes extra time and care to building the parent–teacher relationship in the early years, it can yield rich dividends later on. I even said to the parents in the early years that we would all be challenged by our middle school students later, and now was the time to get to know one another and prepare for the later challenges. Sure enough, when later on some of the students went home with complaints about Mr. Finser, most of the time parents answered, "I know your teacher well. Do as he asks." In a similar fashion, my trust and confidence in the parents allowed for open dialogue and frank conversation on some of the inevitable issues that came our way. They had my back and I had theirs.

Trust and confidence between parents and teachers is the foundation for success in the classroom. It is so important one can rightly call it the "second classroom."

12

Conflict

Despite our best efforts, there are times when we experience conflict, sometimes even in parent–teacher interactions. The instances of this are not so common, in my experience, because most people will do almost anything to avoid conflict. This general tendency is exacerbated in the parent realm, in which most mothers and fathers hold back in expression of any conflict for fear of adverse effects on their child's treatment at school. Thus when it comes to fight or flight, most choose flight. This means swallowing ones words, leaving the scene, and avoiding further discussion. Conflict avoidance is often due to fear of being hurt or hurting others, so feelings are suppressed and one retreats into relative isolation. In a school setting, few will know what is going on other than some may notice that a certain family is not participating the way they used to.

The opposite approach is belligerence, in which a person pursues his or her interests, becomes outspoken in opposition to school policies, and can attempt to steamroll others. Thus I have occasionally come across instances of petitions and letters with many signatures. This is more rare in school situations, and is usually a sign of conflict that has been left unattended for months or even years.

In his book, *Confronting Conflict,* Friedrich Glasl differentiates between social conflicts and differences, making the point that we all have differences, and they are not automatically conflicts. We have differences of perception, feelings, and will impulses, and that makes for a rich tapestry of social life. "So the existence of differences is not the problem, as differences in themselves do not constitute conflict between people. What is important is how people handle their differences and how they experience them."[1]

So when does conflict occur? According to Glasl, a social conflict is a situation where at least one agent or party experiences a difference in a way that his or her ideas, feelings, or intentions are restricted by another agent or party. This experience of restriction gives strength to emerging conflict. This can then grow: "In conflicts, perception is increasingly impaired, so that the people involved in the conflict arrive at different views of reality. Different views in turn lead to more aggression; this increases the differences in perception, intensifies the anger even more and provides the stimuli for further attacks."[2] Attention then becomes more and more selective, threats are perceived more clearly and other things are overlooked, annoying and irritating characteristics of the opponent are noticed and good traits are not recognized. Generally, there is a greater and greater impairment of perception. (See appendices for more on the stages of conflict.)

In another chapter we considered the soul faculties of thinking, feeling, and willing. All three are affected by escalating conflict. Polarized views and ideas arise as perceptions harden, are falsified, muddied, or distorted. Over time the images of the other person harden and one gradually loses sight of the real person. Likewise in the feeling realm, as the armor of insensitivity hardens, the persons in conflict gradually lose sympathy for each other, lose the ability to empathize, and become prisoners of their own emotional state. Moreover, in the will realm, people become biased and paralyzed as the will narrows down the options available and those few possibilities become absolute and radical. Gradually fanaticism takes hold as

---

1   Glasl, *Confronting Conflict*, 17.

2   Ibid., 19.

deeper layers of drives and instincts are awakened. In short, people in conflict change their behavior on many levels.

Because a school is a social organism and a highly visible one at that, conflict between parents, parents and teachers, or teachers and teachers can have devastating consequences. I have seen schools literally ripped apart by unresolved conflict. This often shows itself in dramatic drops in enrollment in an independent school. A school can then enter a descending spiral of budget cuts, fewer programs and positions, less attractiveness for applicants, attrition, even lower enrollment, more budget cuts, and so on. Often a school has to hit a kind of rock bottom in which the pain is so great that everyone, even those not party to the conflict directly, have a vital interest in resolution. Then the will to heal asserts itself and the key players ask for help.

I have also seen schools develop healthy conflict resistance in which over time skills are developed that allow for differences and timely resolution of conflict when it arises. Such schools will have flagging techniques, which make visible the first signs of tensions, and people will be in place in administration to step in early in the game. Leaders should consider it part of their responsibility to monitor tensions and use techniques to assess conflict resistance periodically:

> Staying in touch one-on-one with faculty and staff.
> Regular reporting from different areas of the school.
> Training in giving and receiving feedback.
> Orientation for new faculty, staff, parents.
> Coaching in conflict resolution skills.
> Mentoring systems.
> Complaints committees.
> HR guidelines.
> Supporting administrative staff in their day-to-day management of human situations.

A large part of successful work with conflict is the acceptance of differences, but clarity around decision making is also needed.

Many parents, raised through democratic traditions, assume that if a majority in a class of parents has an opinion, the faculty or administration will agree. They can become frustrated when that is not the case and then they continue to agitate for their point of view. The faculty/staff may then "pull in" behind the walls and retrench. Communication tends to diminish and positions harden.

It would help tremendously if each year the school would renew understandings as to decision making and regularly update the parent handbook. The policies and procedures should be quite explicit, such as:

> Hiring, firing, evaluation of faculty and staff are handled
>   by. . . .
> Decisions on school dress code, calendar, programs are
>   made by. . . .
> The board is responsible for legal and financial decisions.
> The school will consult with parents on changes in the
>   yearly calendar.

Then, with cross-referencing, one can describe the role and authority of all major groups and committees in the school, so everyone knows where to go with an issue or concern.

The administrator and the staff in general play a crucial role in interfacing with parents and making sure that their needs and requests are met. The more one has achieved role clarity the less likely it will be that routine issues escalate to the level of conflict. (More on administration in chapter 20.)

13

Shards of Glass:
When Ideals are Shattered

*M*ost people today have experienced heartbreak of one sort or
another: loss of a friend, the death of a loved one, a divorce,
or professional disappointment. Parents and teachers in Waldorf
schools are not exempt from these or from struggles in general.
Looking in from the outside, some might think that a Waldorf
school is all roses and singing.... There is a lot of that, especially as
children are inherently joyful and optimistic. There is so much that
is good, beautiful, and true in a Waldorf school, and for many, the
years of parenting and teaching at such a school can be deeply fulfilling. However people in Waldorf schools are still people, and as
such are not immune from hardship. Particularly because the ideals
are so high and the potential so great, when things go sour it can be
particularly heart wrenching.

For parents and teachers join Waldorf schools with more than
employment or enrollment in mind. Yes, there is a paycheck, no
matter how modest, and there are enrollment forms to sign, but
the basis of the decision to join such a community of learners often
goes far deeper. Again and again I have heard stories of how the
discovery of a Waldorf school was life changing. Something deep
down in the human soul is touched, the subterranean chords of
a lyre deep within the human psyche start to resonate. Meeting a
Waldorf school is often experienced as a kind of homecoming, a

discovery one has been waiting for over many years. The human heart says "Yes."

The depth of this sounding, the stirring of the inner lyre, can be seen in the amazing dedication that then flows into the lives of parents and teachers. Some might move many miles, assume debt to do teacher training, relocate entire families, or agree to longer commute times as the personal and family universe shifts to align with a new star. As seen in the chapter on life stages of parent involvement, for both parents and teachers there can ensue many years of rich sharing, yearly festivals, friendship, and joy in being with others with similar ideals. In a world with few remaining traditions and rituals, a Waldorf school can be a true community.

Then there are those minor setbacks, which we all experience. I will not go into them here, as they happen in any school, in any life journey. Instead I would like to take a peek at the larger disappointments and what they might mean for parents and teachers. By "larger" I mean the ones that often result in the loss of a teacher or a family, and the silo of silence that often envelopes those departures.

A parent's disappointment with a teacher

As a parent of six children, I have had three occasions in which I had to remove a child from a Waldorf school. With my background in Waldorf education K-10, my many years in teacher education and recently, time spent internationally as an advocate of Waldorf education, the reader can imagine how difficult those decisions were. In one case, my son inherited a teacher who took over the class even though she was burned out, bitter, and cynical. She crushed the children under her sarcasm and hostility. In the second case, the teacher was doing well pedagogically, but the class had serious social cliques and efforts to resolve them were ineffectual. In the third case, the teacher was well meaning but struggled. In two cases we were fortunate to be able to enroll in a nearby Waldorf school; in one situation we sent our daughter to a nearby progressive school. All these instances occurred in elementary schools, and the faculty was unable to deal with the issues in a prompt and decisive manner. Many teachers confided in us that they too saw the problems but were unable to effect changes due to the governance structure and processes at place in the school.

As previously noted parents often serve as the canary in the coalmine, perceiving an issue long before others catch on. Teachers cannot be ruled by the changing opinions of parents, yet they should always listen and ask: can I clear my lenses and look again to see what is really going on? A long time, much valued colleague Arthur Auer looked back on his many years as a member of the college of teachers and said, "We often let someone go two years too late."

It seems that sometimes teachers act as if they fear parents. They want to limit parental influence (and there are instances in which parents overstep their role). Yet fearing parents is like a pilot who fears high altitudes. There are some things that simply come with the job, and if one does not like, or dare I say, enjoy interacting with other adults, perhaps teaching is not the right profession. Teachers cannot retreat behind monastic walls. They need to welcome conversation and a spirit of mutual inquiry. What is best for the children we serve?

Symptoms of fear can include: resisting or limiting the use of parent feedback surveys, having multiple teachers or staff members meet with a "difficult" parent, setting rules such as "don't call me at home" that limit interaction, and phrasing things in vague generalities that frustrate all concerned. One has to have a certain amount of trust, on both sides, to talk straight and say what one really thinks.

Parents need to be aware that they can at times intimidate, not necessarily intentionally, but often by force of personality or profession. A doctor or lawyer in his or her fifties can be overwhelming to a twenty something new teacher. Parents have often learned to get their way at work (or at home) through strength of personality or willpower, and that willfulness can overwhelm a teacher, and not just those in their 20s. Some parents bring a worldly quality of success, professional and financial, that seems to fill the "space" of a class night. They often know how to "manage" people, and understandably can try to transfer these skills to a school situation. They need to look at their own parenting struggles and see that when it comes to child rearing, we are all trying to find a way.

The good news is that all five of our children (one is still in process) graduated from a Waldorf high school, the High Mowing School in Wilton, New Hampshire. Thus they were able to "return," even if to another school. Out of this experience has grown a deep trust in the larger picture of a child's life. As parents we think we can arrange everything to make life good for our children. That is natural. However, each child has his or her own pathway, a trail that must be found. A colleague of more than thirty years, Craig Giddens, once said to me, "Sometimes parents have to follow their children." These words have proven true. This does not mean parents need to respond to every passing whim and wish; rather, seek the deeper meaning of the experiences surrounding our children and learn to adjust accordingly.

A Teacher's Disappointment with a School

When I travel, one of the hardest encounters I meet is when one of my former students, someone who went through the Antioch teacher education program, tells me they are leaving their school. They approach me with an apologetic attitude, as if they are letting me down. And there is often a great deal of anguish and sorrow in such a decision. Again, ideals were shattered.

In some cases, a departure is for reasons of professional competence: classroom management, academics, or the changing needs of the class. Those things are understandable, as are relocations or starting a family. Change is not a bad thing, and for some, it can bring a fresh start and new initiatives. However, for those who leave under troubling circumstances, the transition can test friendships, marriages, and community relations. Sometimes there is a falling out with other colleagues, the administration, or the parents lose confidence in their teacher. Often one experiences a kind of quasi evaluation, in which opinions are formed based on fragments of information. Subjectivity takes over. What could have been handled with mentorship, professional development, and robust evaluation from outside evaluators deteriorates into a trial without jury.

We have to be particularly careful with the snowball effect of subjective parent opinions. I have seen perfectly good teachers who just needed some focused mentoring railroaded out because a few parent voices grew to be the widely held opinion. Often these "few" had a personal agenda; they wanted a teacher to do things in a certain way. They may have seen the teacher as an "employee" subject to their whims. Power and control are often taboo subjects, but they live in all organizations. Parents have been known to use any and every tool they can on behalf of what they perceive to be best for their child. Donors and parent board members need to be especially careful not to wield undue influence on matters that affect one particular grade or program.

For one of the greatest struggles of our time is to take subjective opinions and work toward a more objective basis of working. It is for this reason that I believe in national searches for new hires, outside team evaluators, and active participation in professional bodies such as the Development and Administration Network of AWSNA (DANA), The Alliance for Waldorf Charter Schools, and AWSNA. These groups can share their collective wisdom, attend to best practices, and help raise the bar toward objective processes and policies. Without them, self-administered schools can become schools of self-will and rule by personality.

So what does one do, either as a parent or a teacher when the ideals are shattered? Of course each situation is individual, and there is no "game plan" that fits every instance. How one works with a challenge is as much a matter of right perception and understanding as it is of applying healing modalities. As of this writing I have just begun to learn more about Restorative Justice Circles. However, that will have to wait for a future book. After years of working with both parents and teachers who have gone through "shattered glass" experiences, I have a few suggestions to make:

What burdens the heart needs to find expression in one form or another; it needs release. A painter might do it through color, a musician by playing an instrument, but one art form that is available to all humans today is conversation. It can be harmful to psychological and even physical health if one bottles things up and nurses bitterness. The story needs to be told in order to start the process of letting go. So therefore I urge that within a school community individuals develop social compassion to the point that if someone leaves a school, others reach out to listen and help hold the sorrow. It may not always be wanted, or it might not be the right time, but at least the gesture of reaching out could become part of the social technique of community.

Reaching out with compassion is not only needed by the one who is suffering, but by the whole fabric of the community. Our humanity is made visible not only in joy but also in sorrow.

For the teacher or parent who has left a school, even after some closure conversations, there remains many months, even years of processing. Again, there are no magic pills or solutions, and time does seem to bring about healing gradually. Yet there is one technique that I have found facilitates the inner processing, and that is the three-night exercise recommended by Rudolf Steiner in his karma lectures.[1] Briefly stated, one is advised to form a clear mental picture of the event or situation that occurred. If it was a series of things, one could pick one day or one event that typified the struggle. See the people in your mind's eye; picture the scene as if you were there again. Then take it into sleep so that it can be worked on overnight. Then do it again the second night and a third. Observe yourself upon waking each morning. What happens is that the original event or situation is worked on by the higher members of our being, and transformation occurs (see my book School

---

1   Steiner, *Karmic Relationships*, vol 11, 109–114.

Renewal). *Many people do this unconsciously as a matter of "processing," but if one does this exercise in full consciousness each evening and morning, the transformational process is accelerated.*

We need to learn to perceive what comes into life in the place of what has departed, what now fills the space. Perhaps a whole new occupation opens up, or one realizes one could never have met such and such a friend or partner if one had not gone through the eye of the needle. Look to see what was made possible by having a cathartic experience. Gradually, an acceptance begins to dawn that "this too had a deeper purpose in my life." Gratitude is perhaps going too far, but over time one senses more and more strongly that each child is guided by a star, and that the star never went out, but instead has continued to shine more strongly than ever as a result of the hard changes. Indeed, each of us has a star that guides and supports, but sometimes our vision is blocked by too many clouds.

Through much inner processing, understanding begins to grow. One may never know fully what was at work in the school situation that resulted in the loss, but glimpses may appear. Understanding helps to put things to rest.

For example, in my study of karma and reincarnation, I have come to the view that people have lived previous earthly lives, and that their actions are influenced (not determined) by previous experiences. So let's say that many of those around us lived with each other in the middle ages. Picture what happened in those years: the monastic life, the warring tribes, the castles, betrayal of the Templars, wars over religion, and so on. What if the person, who threw you in the dungeon, separating you from home and family in the 1500s, is now sitting across from you in the parent–teacher conference?

It is not helpful to speculate on these matters, but if we have lived previous lives on Earth, there must be "echoes" that reverberate into the present, and these may play a role is some of our struggles.

I suggest that part of regaining a degree of peace regarding a challenging situation is the perspective that is widened. We see more from the top of a mountain than when we are immersed in the trees below. Spiritual practice and an understanding of karma can help bring perspective.

This little word is so easy to write and so hard to practice: forgiveness. At some point, one has to come to a place of at least a degree of forgiveness if one wants truly to move on. For me it often is associated with a kind of return to the original reasons why one connected to a school, the wonderful people that came into one's life as a consequence, and the lasting value of the whole experience. After time, and what I call "consciously willed forgiveness" one can come to a place where one can say to the players in the drama, "go in peace, for I wish you well." If one is able to forgive, some release is possible.[2]

When all is really over, and one has moved on, there is a danger that one simply forgets. My Mom always used to say, "I can forgive but I cannot forget." Although it is tempting to drink the draught of forgetfulness, it is not terribly helpful in the long run. Some of the shards need to be washed out to sea, but others can return as smooth glass, even sparkling in the sun. How can one let the sea do its work? I have found that discovering the essence of the experience, the core question that was at the heart of the challenge, is such a transformation. Instead of blaming, accusing, constantly relating what went wrong, one can gradually come to a place where one can distill everything down to a real question or two. The question one arrives at is not abstract, theoretical, or intellectual, but instead is forged through the fire of lived experience. Those questions can move worlds. Here are a few examples from my "lived experience" in Waldorf schools:

---

2   In this regard, I highly recommend Sergei O. Prokofieff's book *The Occult Significance of Forgiveness.*

Why was my child placed in that classroom with that teacher at that time in his or her life?

Why do schools dedicated to self-administration struggle so much with human resource management, self-evaluation, and self-governance?

If a school has a biography that goes through phases as happens in the life of an individual, what does it mean to be part of one phase or another? Why was I there at that time?

Why did those key "players" in that painful event/situation find each other on that stage? What were they "asking" of each other?

If there is such a thing as reincarnation, what remains unresolved for the key "players" to be worked on in the future?

Do we need to have periods of darkness to appreciate the light more?

Why do so many of us only "wake up to each other" when in crisis?

The list could go on and on, but I urge my readers to form distilled questions, for they can help turn experiences into productive forces for further living. Like the old fairy tale of spinning straw into gold, if one can "turn" an experience into a question, good can become of what was truly painful.

For something else happens with the asking of questions that are forged from hard living: our star becomes brighter, and our angel listens. Yes, whether using the Socratic term "daemon" or the phrase "higher self" or the transcendent I, there are many ways of expressing what countless people have experienced as their angel at work.[3] *And that being does not feed on physical nourishment; it needs our questions. Thus life with all its hardships for both parents and teachers in the end serves a greater purpose. Like iron, we are*

---

3 See my father Siegfried Finser's book, *Footprints of an Angel.*

forged through life into servant leaders who, through our greater compassion and understanding, are able to do so much more for humanity.

It was a great pleasure when my wife and I met Gordon Walmsley and his wife Annie Borre at a little café on the coast of the Baltic Bornholm in summer 2013. The four of us had a long afternoon conversation, the kind that is possible when on vacation. Some weeks later they sent us a box of books, including Gordon's wonderful poetry. I would like to end this chapter with a portion of one of his poems as he so beautifully captures much of what I have tried to share in this chapter:

> *I am told that angels*
> *And all beings of the Sun*
> *And of all the unseen worlds*
> *Must answer*
> *Questions we urge on them*
> *But that there is one condition:*
> *That the questions be real.*
> *Real questions must be forged*
> *Fired to just the right heat*
> *Plunged into rivers of ice.*
> *Thus it is our questions must be forged*
> *In fire and ice*
> *Because if a question*
> *Doesn't have*
> *The right heat*
> *No angel can hear it.*
> *I believe that, say it many times*
> *In many ways, and find it to be true*
> *Not because someone told me*
> *But because I have tested it*
> *Letting it resonate*
> *in chambers*

consecrated to me
and you
long long ago
before the time when questions
could grow, as now
into sacraments
and when I think about this –
about the many-colored marvel
of the question
think of it
as a glowing bridge
spanning our world
and a world of beings
possibly unseen.[4]

Our questions are bridges to one another and to the spiritual world.

---

4   Portion of the poem *Touchstones* by Gordon Walmsley.

14

Dance of the Shadows

*W*hen *we meet someone, we are introduced, or we have to introduce ourselves. We do so by saying our name, often also shaking hands. In group situations, such as parent evenings, there are many creative ways to do introductory games and break the ice. Once we know each other by first name, we feel more comfortable and over time we relax into the relationship. It is much easier to return into a group of parents or teachers where one knows most of the people than it is to walk into a room full of strangers. We are lulled into the illusion that we know one another.*

Yet do we? Do we have any idea of the life story, the joy and sorrow a person has experienced? We may find out where someone went to school, but it might be a while before we find out that one couple almost lost their first child, or that another is struggling with a new job. The mystery of "who are you?" is one that life reveals to us over time.

Along the way, we alternate between periods of sleep and waking, not literally, but in relation to those around us in the parent evening, for instance. As we listen to others, there is a tendency to be taken along for the ride, lulled into "I know what she is going to say about field trips..." and in our consciousness we fall asleep to the person speaking. Then something happens, a disagreement or a new person joins the group, and we wake up again. Suddenly we see things in a new light. Our social life is full of this alternating cycle of waking and sleeping in regard to others around us.

A crisis or conflict is the ultimate wake-up call. It is often a moment when all those concerned awake at the same time. Everyone starts to focus. Suddenly we realize we didn't really know the people around us!

This is because our everyday selves, or everyday ego, is normally masked by all sorts of social conventions. "He is a sixth grade parent with another child in the second grade and works at the local bank." We were content to know this, until the wake-up call. Then suddenly we see that, behind the mask of the everyday self, there is a person with struggles and tensions, a person working with the polarities of Light and Shadow, a conscious life and a less conscious life. The real personality of the person starts to emerge. So one might say, conflict, or at least some struggle, has a very useful purpose in human evolution.

But we know from Anthroposophy that a person is not just what we experience in the everyday sense as a personality. Each one of us also has a Higher Self that contains our strengths and aspirations as a human being. Here we have achieved some understanding of ourselves, our life goals, ideals, and values. We have made some choices in life and when they were made out of the Higher Self they were fully conscious and aligned with our destiny. In a crisis, the higher selves of people around us often emerge for the first time, and it is good. We see with new eyes the tremendous human potential, the vast resources available to the school!

There is a third aspect to the human being as well, as Fredriech Glasl mentions in his book Confronting Conflict: *the shadow personality, or double. Here we discover negative characteristics, weaknesses—our splinter personality. The word "splinter" is apt: thoughts, feelings, and will/actions have disconnected and we can be like a three-headed monster at times. We project our failings on others, and we interpret the actions of others in a negative light.*[1]

---

1   Glasl, *Confronting Conflict*, 31.

In my work with schools I have found that organizations some-times go through a perfect storm. Just at the time of a budget crunch, or a personnel crisis, the school is subject to a dance of the shad-ows. The untransformed, less conscious aspects of key individu-als emerges in a macabre dance, feeding off the shadow images of the others. They may not all be dancing under the moonlight, but sometimes it feels that way.

What can be done in such a situation? A course of action (or intervention if one is a consultant) varies based upon the case at hand, but in general, the first step is to hold up a mirror and move from confrontation of the other to self-confrontation. In my assess-ment interviews, I often ask for "the story" followed by, "What has been your role in this narrative?" Then eventually to, "If you could go back in time, would you have done things differently?" These kinds of questions promote self-reflection and self-assessment, a key ingredient in group/organizational change. I often work with individuals before taking on large-group exercises.

Then in terms of the larger group or organization, I might find an occasion to ask them to list patterns of behavior that have held them back and ones that they aspire to. So on one column they might write: indirect talking about each other in the hallway or teachers room. On the other side of the chart they might say: talk-ing directly to the person concerned. Out of this we develop some Rules of the Road, or group norms. After the list is completed, I ask if there are some that need clarification. When that is done, turning to the forward-looking list I ask, is there anything on this list you do not agree with? Usually there is none, if we have done the clarifi-cations thoroughly. Then, much to their surprise I ask, Do we have agreement that these are qualities we aspire to for our interactions going forward? *The consensus on this piece often comes as a tre-mendous surprise to a group that has been at odds.... "What! We all agreed to something!" And with a small step forward we have started to step back into the Light pole of the organization and the shadows have had to pull back a bit.*

For this is the central task of group work: how can we help each individual, each parent and teacher, stand in his or her light in service of the whole? Not someone else's light, but their own, with all the shades of color and difference that makes each person such an untold story. By coming together we can embark on a voyage of discovery, and together do what no one of us could do alone. With group processes and facilitation skills that are honed like a well-tuned musical instrument, it is possible to reach a place in which each person finds their rightful role, just as each musician has a separate instrument to play in an orchestra. However we need a common score, the mission of the organization, and the aspirations in the Light pole to keep us together. It can be done, and when we are successful, the music is pleasing for all to hear.

Parents Have Needs, Too

Parents enroll their children in a school so they can receive a good education. Of course, this is the foremost reason for parent involvement in a school, and much of their day-to-day activity revolves around the needs of their children. Yet over the years of working with Waldorf schools, I have found that there is a subtle, more delicate aspect of parent involvement. Many, at first often unconsciously, are drawn to a Waldorf school with their own striving, their own search for meaning in life. Many parents spend long hours at work performing, in some cases, tasks that are routine. Some hold onto jobs for the sake of health insurance or the regular paycheck long after their hopes and aspirations have moved on. I am so impressed with the spirit of sacrifice of some, who continue doing things all day long so their children can have the benefit of a good education. Of course, there are many jobs out there that are fulfilling, but parenting is in itself a path of sacrifice on one level or another. Thus it is for many, that when they discover a Waldorf school for their children, they also find a possibility for a new community for the whole family, and a place where adults can meet one another in a new way.

Parents seek renewal and strength through their association with a Waldorf school. Some find it through the festivals, others through conversation with other parents, and some want to engage in self-development, inspired by the example of some of the wonderful teachers and other parents they meet in the school. This is a most subtle aspect of school life, in that one has to leave everyone free in terms of individual spiritual life. One cannot impose on the inner, sacred sanctuary that comprises the Self of another human being. Thus, one has to wait for a question to arise. A discussion of a PTO and other more outer forms would not be complete without mentioning this aspect as well. It is part of the revealed mystery of community. People are drawn together out of a mutual desire to evolve. This is a potent force behind a school. Just as the sap rising in New Hampshire maple trees in the spring is a reality—and a sweet one for those who like maple syrup!—so the forward-looking, self-actualization force in a striving human being can become a resource for health in a school community. Our striving provides nourishment for a school.

> *In mystery, what I received*
> *To sheathe within my memory,*
> *Be further meaning of my striving:*
> *In gaining strength it shall awaken*
> *The forces of my self within;*
> *Evolving, give myself to me.*[2]

---

2   Steiner, *Calendar of the Soul*, verse 19.

15

Why Parent Organizations Are so Difficult to Sustain

In the Waldorf schools I visit, there is always a board of trustees, a faculty, and often a college of teachers, but often the parent organization comes and goes (see more on teacher-led administration later). There are years when a few key parents enthusiastically lead a parent–teacher organization (PTO), and then the energy seems to wane, things languish, meetings are sparsely attended, and the few who attend wonder why they are meeting. Then, after some time, a new impulse arises and others step forward to repeat the cycle. This transitory nature of parent organizations has long puzzled me, and it has contributed to the uncertainties around the parent role in a school.

A board of trustees has a defined role, and the parents who serve on that group seem to have considerable clarity as to roles and responsibilities. A board by law (501c3) is financially and legally responsible for the affairs of the school. That gives the board real tasks for the development, safety, and delegation of pedagogical policies to the faculty and staff as well as passing the budget. One area of concern from my experience serving on seven boards over the years is the notion of a "parent representative" on the board. I find this term a misnomer; one is either a trustee or not. In any case, how can a person possibly represent 300 parents? Most of the individuals who have held this role end up just representing themselves.

Gradually, more and more schools have come to the view that one is first and foremost a trustee, with responsibility to make decisions for the good of the whole school, not just the parents. This means that every trustee should play a role in fundraising and certainly contribute to the annual fund. Thus, I recommend that schools do away with the term "parent representative" on the board and simply draw from the community those individuals most capable to serve.

Which brings us back to parent organizations as the rightful "home" for parent-to-parent work, as well as an expression of the parent "voice" in school matters. Parents need to find one another in a context other than the class nights, which naturally centers on the children and the teachers. Parents need to share common issues around child rearing, curriculum and school policies, and if the PTO also has a "T"—that is, teachers present—one has a wonderful opportunity for conversation.

So why do parent organizations come and go? I feel it is due to the lack of a clear vision or mission, irregular attendance, and especially the lack of real tasks. Because the parent-focused organization is so vital to the health of the parent–teacher relationship over all, I would like to take up each of these three aspects separately.

Vision and Mission

Why have a PTO? In carrying the tasks of the school, there is a role for a PTO distinct from that of the board or the faculty and staff. It involves what one might call the cultural and social life of the adult community. This involves an educational component, knowing something of the philosophy and curriculum of the school, but also creating a space for questions that are not child or grade specific. Parents need a place to discuss, for example, festivals, assemblies, dress code, attendance expectations, and community relations. The cultural life of a school is connected to that of the community, so networking with other nonprofits can be ever so valuable, and parents are the best link to the wider community. One parent might be on the board of the local theater; another might be connected to the museum or local college. Such parents become a resource for the faculty in planning field trips and to the board in terms of friend raising and fundraising. The goal of a PTO is community building, both internally to the school and externally. This can be enhanced through specific tasks:

The Tasks of a PTO

- Welcome and orientation of new parents, staff, and faculty
- Conversation on school-wide topics of mutual interest
- Networking with community organizations
- Supporting festivals, school assemblies and school-wide gatherings with logistics, food, music. and warmth
- Raising money for special projects
- Asking the questions that need the attention of faculty, staff, or board
- Being "an ear" for current issues in the parent body and the community
- Nominating capable individuals to serve on committees of the school
- Assisting with recruitment and outreach efforts
- Hosting special events, such as grandparents' day and faculty appreciation day

Attendance

All this is possible if one has a reliable group to work with. I have seen many ways schools have attempted to ensure regular attendance, and the one I liked best was a system of each class—nursery, kindergarten, grades 1 to 12—electing two class representatives to the PTO. These folks would be required to attend PTO meetings, whereas the other parents are warmly encouraged. However, with a base of 26 reps in attendance, they would then elect a chair and vice chair to serve in a leadership role. These two would form the agendas, invite speakers, make sure the faculty, staff, and board designate someone to give reports and prepare the social and snack side of the meeting. One needs to foster a sense that real topics are being taken up, that the conversations matter, and valuable tasks are performed on behalf of the school.

I once participated in a parent organization in which the group was responsible for raising money for special projects. Thus if new playground equipment was needed, or risers for the chorus, the PTO would take this on. They later enjoyed the attendant satisfaction of seeing the results of their work in a visible way. Otherwise fundraising by parents, such as for the fall fair, can be seen as going into what some say is the never-ending "black hole" of the school budget. Parents need to see visible results as well as support the annual giving campaign for the sake of the overall school. This combination of special projects and annual giving seems to strike the right balance. It gives the PTO concrete tasks, which ground the work in reality. When it is real, people attend.

Thus, with a clear mission, regular attendance and specific tasks, a PTO has a chance to make valuable contributions to a school. If the faculty and staff have confidence in the work of this organization, it is advisable to have the chair and vice chair meet with the school's overall executive leadership team once a month to coordinate agendas and compare notes. One then starts to approach what one could call a collaborative leadership model of school governance.

16

The Life Cycle of Parent Involvement in a School

Most teachers, not just in Waldorf schools, have studied various child development models. From Erikson to Piaget, teachers consider the various stages of development as a basis for applying the curriculum most effectively. It is rare that a teacher education course does not cover human development, though our modern mindset of "teach for the test" seems to diminish the importance of these considerations, much to the detriment of our children.

Parents, indeed all adults, also go through life cycle changes. For a while there was even a raft of popular literature on this subject (*Passages* by Gail Sheehy among others). There is of course relevance to the issue of adult development in terms of human relations. It makes a difference to the parent–teacher relationship if, as was the case when I started out as a teacher, the parents I worked with were all old enough to be my parents! Later on I felt more like I was with contemporaries, and then of course, that changed as well. Those in their twenties see the world differently from someone in their mid-fifties. This is all a matter of common sense.

However, the aspect that most fascinates me is the notion that parents go through stages of development in their relationship to their child's school. If I am on the right track with this, such a developmental process could have tremendous implications for the teacher–parent relationship. What could these stages look like?

Discovery. This stage includes the first encounter with the school, the admissions process and early months of enrollment. It is characterized by wonder, surprise, and even amazement. We may hear in Waldorf schools statements, "I had no idea this place existed. I wish I could have been a child at this school. This is fabulous!" Parents at this stage are incredulous, eager to learn more, and full of enthusiasm.

Conviction. As they emerge from the discovery process many parents in a Waldorf school enter the stage of firm conviction. This stage can last one to three years. Everyone in the extended family ends up hearing about their child's school, as well as neighbors and anyone else willing (and sometimes not so willing) to listen. Parents often seem to have become overnight experts on the curriculum, and they relate stories of festivals and parent evenings. The school can do no wrong. It is from this group that many recruits to committees and even the board and PTO can be found.

It is not unusual to find a majority of the activist parents coming from this segment of the parent body, which has implications for school governance. On the one hand such an enthusiastic cadre is a great asset for the school in terms of volunteerism and getting things done. (More on this subject in the chapter on the Uber-Volunteer.) Yet the unwavering enthusiasm can deter those who have a question or an issue from stepping forth. One is either a "believer" or not, and an honest question can be seen as disrespectful. School administrators have to be particularly attentive to inclusion and group process to counteract this tendency.

This stage of conviction is also characterized by high expectations and what Glasl calls "positive idolization."[1] This is a great asset in pioneering ventures, as one has unity around common ideals and people see the best in each other. Negative qualities are overlooked and people just see the "light" aspects, and conflict is seen as inconceivable.

---

1   Glasl, *Conflict*, 49.

Testing. For some, this occurs gradually, as one begins to see the odd weakness in a teacher or another parent, or some of the meetings do not go as well as expected. In other cases, the first instances of testing can come around the curriculum when, for instance, a parent is unsatisfied with questions about reading or a social situation. In a few cases there is a serious "fall from paradise" in which disappointments accumulate and the "positive idolization" can turn, almost overnight, into "negative idolization." The shadow sides of people emerge, and the ideals are tested.

This fall from grace can be especially acute in organizations with high spiritual ideals, such as church groups, civic organizations, ecologically oriented protest movements and Waldorf schools. When the ideals are so high, the disappointment around unmet expectations can be much more damaging.

Organizations would do well to prepare better for this stage of testing when parents are still in the discovery and conviction stages. This can be done by outlining the possible stages of involvement ahead of time and anticipating some of the more predictable questions as part of an orientation process.

Commitment. From a period of testing arises a new, more grounded stage we might call commitment. Parents still carry the ideals, but they are now balanced with a certain element of realism. About the teacher who used to "walk on water," one might now hear, "He is also a human being, after all." The strength of the curriculum and the fact that the children are learning and seem happy will carry the day. When those parents join committees, the board and PTO can become the backbone of the school and be counted on to "deliver the goods," whether it is chairing the fall fair, writing a financial appeal letter, or serving on the recruitment committee. Their views are believable, carry weight, and the school trusts them.

Outer orbits. This is a hard stage to characterize, as it takes many different forms and is not particularly dramatic. In my experience, what happens is that, as parents and their children get older, say now in the middle school, the parents get more tied up in work, community organizations, and the children are no longer so eager to see their parents hanging around the school all the time. This combination of factors means that some parents "fade"; they are less present. If questioned, they will still attest to the value of the school and even jump in to help from time to time, but now they are more selective. In some cases, parents continue to be loyal supporters of their child's particular class, but not for the school as a whole. In other cases, they simply take turns and show up less frequently. How a school handles this phase is crucial for the high school. If there are guilt trips and admonitions, expectations that cannot be met, some parents will continue to pull back until they no longer enroll their child. This drop off can occur most often after sixth or eighth grade. When my first son was in seventh grade, I took a break after four years of service on the board, including one year as the board president. I received a call from a new parent (in the conviction stage) who wanted me to work at the fall fair. When I said I would be unable to participate because of a road trip, she said something like, "Parents like you make more work for the rest of us." Of course, she did not know about my four years on the board, which I then explained. This again raises the issue of volunteer management and institutional memory. If on the other hand the school is able to help parents navigate through this stage of outer orbits, there can be rich rewards. I suggest that the administration leave parents be at this stage; like a homing pigeon, there is a high chance the flight path will bring them back into a more active relationship with the school.

A school needs a person or group that carries some "institutional memory," so that there is mindfulness of the life cycle of parent involvement and a greater acceptance of these natural changes in involvement. These stages need to be discussed as part of parent orientation.

Return. One of the greatest challenges high schools face is that they often have parents either in the outer orbit stage or on the return path. I sometimes see my high school colleagues wistfully eyeing the early-childhood parents who bring such unabashed idolization and enthusiasm to school events. Yet "the gods of enrollment" are often kind to high schools, in that there are some students who arrive from another school, and their parents, though not identical because of age differences, do bring some of the qualities of the aforementioned stages. Moreover, the involvement of the parent on the "return stage" can also be a wonderful thing to work with. These folks, by and large, know what they are doing, why they are there, and they have found ways to balance life and school volunteerism. They may not be at the school very much, but when they make a commitment to do something, they usually follow through with grace and considerable skill. The parents of older students have also learned from life and can apply their wisdom to schools that are willing to engage them in projects.

Lifelong gratitude. These are the alumni parent years—the "golden pond years." Some schools have found ways to work with alum parents; others are still in process. These folks can be a literal gold mine for the school, and not just financially. I have known alum parents who return and serve another term on the board, who help with outreach, and who participate in panel discussions on the educational program their children received. These former parents are credible. They are able to speak out of both theory and experience, with wonderful anecdotes to liven things up. Together, they form a living sheath of protection around a school.

Alumni–parent relations should be one of the highest priorities of any school.

Together, these stages constitute a remarkable journey. It would be wonderful to have more parent stories of the twelve to fourteen years they have spent accompanying their child through elementary and secondary years. It is a path, a true schooling for the parents as well as their children.

Let us open up spaces for conversation between parents in PTO meetings and class nights, alum parent reunions and conferences so these issues become discussable. We need national conferences just for parents, a blog, and interactive webinars so the conversations can flourish.

When teachers, staff, and parents can work from the consciousness of stages of parent involvement, it is more likely that the community will remain intact and that challenges will be greeted with compassion rather than condemnation.

To know that certain stages are "normal" is to accept, empathize, and engage. These human qualities are what make a school a community.

17

The Problem of Evil

In a course I teach at Antioch University called Evolving Consciousness, we look at the big picture of human evolution in relation to ancient civilizations and the changes in human consciousness through history. At one point in the course we usually take a break from our usual format to have what we call a Goethean conversation on the theme of evil. For those who do not know this format, Marjorie Spock (sister of Dr. Benjamin Spock) brought out a pamphlet on the art of Goethean conversation, which basically is a prepared topic with clear guidelines as to layering the contributions. Each person tries to refer back to at least one of the previous comments, thus building a common thread in the conversation. The class is given a week to consider several questions, such as: What is evil? How do we know something is evil? Where does it come from? Can something evil become good or vice versa? On the appointed day we rearrange the furniture to get out from behind desks and make a circle with our chairs. The students are told that silence is a friend of conversation and that in the Quaker style; it is ok to have times of contemplation and deep listening. Then we begin.

I cannot hope to replicate the many wonderful perspectives that come from my graduate students in such an exercise, but I do want to allocate a few paragraphs to the theme of evil in history and our time. For it seems that as far back as Cain and Abel, humanity has been grappling with this topic, and yet it remains unfortunately modern. One has only to turn on CNN, *or especially the local news channels to get the latest version.*

Much of our struggle as humans on this Earth has been to find our humanity in the face of evil. Something that might have worked for a particular culture at a particular time such as the caste system in India is no longer acceptable or appropriate today. Time and again in mythology and folklore from around the world, stories are told of efforts to overcome evil, to divert evil into something that serves rather than destroys. It seems that human beings continue to be faced with myriad temptations, and that a significant segment of the population continues to surrender to these temptations through which evil can enter. And all too often adversity is met with more evil, the whole "eye for an eye" phenomena. It is as if human vision of the higher ideals is clouded from time to time in history, and evil is allowed to work its will on humanity.

Steiner spoke of 1879 as a decisive year in which "spirits of darkness" were released to become even more active within human impulses, especially the faculty of reason. Thus human beings became even more susceptible to the "obscure errors."[1] But the year 1879 also marks a positive moment in that increased spiritual wisdom also began to flow into human beings, and for those who take up the challenge, it is possible that through thinking one can bring new spiritual strength to human actions. Confusion in the human soul can be resolved through inner activity.

Steiner goes on to say that in the fourth cultural epoch, the Greco/Roman time, the struggle of humanity was to comprehend the Mystery of Golgotha, but that now, in the fifth cultural epoch, the human soul seeks to learn how, with the help of Christ, to transform evil into good. Rather than have "the good" decreed from on high, as in some ancient cultures, each human being today has to find the inner battle, and out of personal freedom, find a way to transform evil into good. Every human encounter, every challenge

---

1   Steiner, *Secret Brotherhoods*, 164.

we face can be met in a way we choose, and sometimes the smallest struggles are actually significant stepping stones on the collective path from evil to good.

In an earlier chapter on the Foundation Stone meditation, I developed the idea of the threefold human being as full of potential for harmony and constructive work in building a community of parents, teachers, and children. I cited three so-called "panels" or verses, and hinted at a fourth. This last one fits well in the context of transforming evil into good, in that it speaks eloquently of the "turning point in time" referred to by Rudolf Steiner as a crucial moment in human history:

> At the turning point of time
> The Spirit-light of the world
> Entered the stream of Earth existence.
> Darkness of night
> Had ceased its reign;
> Day-radiant light
> Shone forth in human souls:
> Light
> That gives warmth to simple shepherds' hearts;
> Light
> That enlightens the wise heads of kings.
> Light divine
> Christ-Sun
> Warm our hearts
> Enlighten our heads;
> That good may become
> What from our hearts
> We are founding,
> What from our heads we direct
> With focused will.

One thing that I have found invaluable is a basic question: does this thought, feeling, or action enhance the humanity, the *spirit essence of the other person, or does it dampen and obscure it? Where the human spirit is supported, and by spirit I mean the free expression of the individual in the higher self (see chapter 2, "Self-less-ness"), there we have the possibility for good to become. Conversely, in those who have been most hell-bent on evil—figures such as Hitler and Stalin—we find a decapitation of the spirit, or individual. Through sleep deprivation and certain interrogation techniques, victims are robbed of their humanity under oppressive regimes. When we become abstract categories, and see each other as stereotypes, as objects, we de-humanize. When we look to the striving of the individual, the search for the universal human, we are winning a victory for the good.*

Each moment in the day of a parent or a teacher is an opportunity to win a victory for humanity. The struggle of good to overcome evil is not decided on the battlefield anymore (if it ever was) but now, more than ever, the outcome depends on the nature of each and every human encounter.

18

The Veteran Teacher

O f course, teachers go through stages of development as well.
But rather than focus on that aspect here as there is now much
material available through the literature on mentoring, I would like
to look at one segment of the profession that is often overlooked: the
very experienced teacher. In the rush to improve teacher education
programs, strengthen mentoring and professional development, the
attention has often been riveted on beginning teachers, and indeed
this book began with them in focus for the first chapter. But what
are the issues and needs of teachers who have been in the classroom
for 10, 20, even 30 or more years? I am also keen on this group
because they often play a major, decisive role in school administration and parent relations. In a Waldorf school, these are the folks
who are expected to not only mentor new teachers, but also serve
as committee chairs, faculty chair, college chair, and give talks to
parents and the community at public functions. How is it with these
veteran teachers? Who even asks this question?

The Gifts of Experience

Thanks to years in the classroom, many of these colleagues are a
walking treasure trove of wisdom. There is little they do not know!
They have been through many ups and downs in the history of their
school, some have taught at other schools, and this real-life experience informs their decision making in matters large and small. They

also know how to navigate through the organization, which people to talk with before a meeting, and how to problem solve. They are often unstinting in their service, sometimes to an extreme so that one wonders if there is much time for a personal life. Even schools with less than adequate structures and procedures somehow manage to survive thanks to the extraordinary efforts of this generation of teachers. Through sheer strength of personality, these experienced colleagues can make things work, even at the risk of being seen as an oligarchy.

The Personal Sacrifices

Because of their great dedication to the affairs of the school, one has to wonder sometimes if these colleagues have a life. One sometimes sees a spouse or partner at a school event, but it is rather exceptional. Their own children may have moved on to college or beyond, so there is less interaction with other parents on that level. Preparation for classes is still needed, but they know how to focus and efficiently determine which materials are needed for each subject. Many have at least the veneer of outer self-assurance and confidence, but if one looks closely or engages in conversation, one can sense a subtle disquiet at times.

Career Issues

There is very little upward mobility in the teaching profession. Unless one goes into administration or higher education, many veteran teachers can feel as if they have hit a glass ceiling professionally as well as economically. There is satisfaction to be had from mentoring, and also from serving in school leadership roles, but after a certain number of years doing that, then what?

There is an international need to look at the teaching profession from a career perspective, especially in regard to our most experienced teachers. Can we pool our resources, for example, to create a pre-retirement professional group of roving mentors who could be called upon to visit schools that need help? Can we create service apprentice programs for new teachers that would be run by long-serving colleagues? What about research fellowships? Visiting scholar programs at teacher training colleges?

We need to be at least asking these questions and forming proposals to address the life cycle issues of our experienced colleagues.

The stronger the light, the greater the shadows.

Failure to address these issues could result in unacceptable alternatives, which sometimes already play themselves out in our schools. What follows are a few of the possible symptoms. Veteran teachers can be unapproachable at times owing to their formidable presence and stature within the school community. This may not be their fault and, indeed, as a teacher/professor for 35 years, I have had to ask myself these questions and sometimes the "unapproachable" stance can be mostly a matter of perception. Nevertheless, it can become an issue for parent–teacher relations.

Some long-time teachers, as in any profession, become set in their ways.

Questions and requests for discussion can be met with shut down responses such as, "This is how we handle recess at our school." Full stop. End of discussion. Attempts to bring up the topic in the future meet with similar responses and lo and behold, even if one goes through the proper channels for agenda planning, it never ends up on the agenda. It has been successfully blocked behind the scenes.

Self-interest can enter the equation in a profession that is known for its altruism. One can understand the anxiety of a teacher who will soon retire, who has worked for years with little or no pension plan, and has just social security to count on. Self-interest is an insidious thing once it enters the social organism. One long-time teacher who had long defended the school's sabbatical policy persuaded the board (many members of which had had children in her classes) to give her a lump sum cash payment instead of a sabbatical. She did not get the break from teaching that many thought was needed, and life style choices were made that many questioned. All schools need conflict of interest and nepotism policies, as well as standard procedures around when and how to recuse oneself from a decision-making body. Almost all people I know have self-interests; it is human. The issue becomes particularly potent however when someone has the influence to bend organizational decision making at will.

Many long-time teachers exercise considerable power and authority without accepting formal roles in these later stages of their career. Instead, these individuals become informal leaders who rule behind the throne, so to speak. I have sometimes asked these folks why they refuse formal leadership roles and the answers are usually evasive. So I just observe. The result, however harsh it may sound, is that I think some want it this way because informal leaders are not held accountable. A formal leader, such as a school chair or board president, is usually evaluated regularly and there are terms of office built into the bylaws. Informal leaders are in many ways "above the law," and they can influence decisions with relative impunity.

Senior faculty and staff have to also guard against undue influence on board members, faculty, and staff, many of whom they helped hire. By selectively sharing information, even parents can be influenced to lobby for a cause. Often the issue at hand is quite innocuous, such as recess policy, but the successful defense of such a position enhances the aura of invincibility that is part of the power base of such a senior person.

A senior teacher can at times bring to bear influence that goes far beyond the ordinary. This cannot be exercised too often or questions will arise, but when done selectively, it can be very effective. I have seen how high schools and other new programs are started almost single-handedly because of one unstoppable advocate. Advocacy is not a bad thing, but a premature birth without the medical team on board can be dangerous to the health of the social organism when the strong-willed advocate(s) have not won at least some measure of consensus from the entire organization.

Finally, one has to watch for the phenomena of senior faculty that form a nucleus, a kind of "captains quarters" that endures through thick and thin. I knew a school that had essentially the same core group of five to seven faculty/staff over thirty years as younger faculty came and went. The toll on mid-level faculty/staff was particularly severe, as they often pounded their heads against the door without admittance. A school pays a heavy price for letting such a nucleus develop, not only for social reasons, but also for when they retire; it often creates an existential crisis for the entire school.

One might ask at this point, "What does all this have to do with the second classroom and parent–teacher relations? In a general sense, if something is not well in one part of the body social, it affects all the other organs. But more specifically—a king or queen of the faculty is not necessarily the best person to serve as king or queen of parent and or community relations. To put it simply, although there is of course some overlap, different skill sets are needed. Parents need school leaders who are accessible, empathetic, open to questions, willing to reconsider policy, sincere, and as objective as possible. That can be the case with a senior teacher. All I am saying is that it is not automatic.

Schools that continually select leaders based just on the internal dynamics of the organization put themselves at risk. Leaders need to face outward as well as inward.

Parents generally do not have the time to untangle the internal dynamics of school administration. They need clear, open pathways to access information. Administrators and those who are not in the classroom can play a vital role in this regard (see chapter on Administration).

Without any intent, experienced teachers can sometimes be intimidating in a way that stops less confident parents from asking questions. The problem with the unasked question is that one never knows about the missed opportunity. A parent may inadvertently be blocked from moving up the stages of parental involvement as described earlier, or might internalize assumptions that later emerge in conflict.

Over time, the tone and character of a school can take on aspects of the lead teacher(s) personality. This can be a good thing, such as "the school where they make great music" or it can result in advance sorting, a condition in which potential applicants do not even inquire due to the perceptions living in the community.

Advanced sorting happens both with new student enrollment and recruitment of new faculty. When too pervasive, a school can become an island of like-minded individuals.

In any profession it is essential to stay up to date on the latest research. It is interesting that it is often the younger and mid-career teachers who most readily flock to seminars on social inclusion and working with children with special needs. Most teachers are lifelong learners, but some just get too tired to attend conferences and workshops. Old patterns and attitudes then go unchallenged.

In the end, our schools need and should value veteran teachers for what they can give, and at the same time be aware of the ramifications of asking too much of the same people. As with many things in life, the solution rests in balance, bringing on new, younger teachers who have fresh impulses into the school, and valuing the mid-career teachers who are ready to step up and take more responsibility. Leadership succession does not happen automatically, and some planning and discussion on these themes can go a long way toward sustainability. I urge schools to at least put the topic of succession on the agenda, look at it together, and begin to formulate a plan.

A veteran teacher is often one who has achieved many insights, is able to see truths and communicate them to new colleagues. But if we are a real community, we need to embrace the needs of all members, and find ways to effect graceful transitions.

19

Round Churches

*A*church has traditionally been a place of worship, and the
architecture has evolved through centuries. How a church, or
any building for that matter is designed, speaks to the view of the
human being at that time in history as well as the nature of the
activity within. The Gothic gesture, of stretching for the heavens,
is very different from the Romanesque, for instance. The pyramid
has in many ways the opposite gesture of a Greek temple. The former is directed down toward the Earth while the later rises above
in balance with gravity and the cosmos. So it was with particular
interest that in August 2014 that I once again visited the four round
churches on the Baltic island of Bornholm.

What is the experience of being in a round church? The Ols kirke, for instance, not only has round walls, but also is supported from within by a large round pillar at the center. The large stones that pave the floor are arranged in circular patterns around that central pillar, and the interior roof is rounded, with the highest point at the center. Drawings have been discovered under the plaster of the interior roof, and the drawings are mostly plant forms, speaking of the life force of the Christ. Hanging from the roof inside is a wooden model sailing ship, the vessel of the community present in many Danish churches.

If one walks around the exterior of the Ols kirke, one is at first struck by the fact that near the foundation there are places where the structure juts out for support (buttresses), so the base is not perfectly round. We are, of course, also creatures of the Earth. But as one gazes up the exterior walls, past some of the small inset windows, one then sees how the white walls become fully circular as they extend upward. The roof is like an upside down ice cream cone, again perfectly circular. The gardens around the church are immaculate (again circular), with many flowering shrubs and even some blackberries inviting to be picked. Although relatively small, the Ols kirke leaves a deep impression on the visitor. (See picture.)

What lived in the imagination of those who built the four round churches on Bornholm? Did the Knights Templar really flee to Bornholm? Did they inspire the churches? Did they bury their treasures there? And how do the round churches speak to us today?

It suddenly struck me that the circle, so often repeated in these structures, is the symbol of completion, of unity. The spiritual worlds and the Earth are one in the Ols kirke. Within the church, I felt complete harmony. Thinking, feeling, and willing were reunited, and a human being could find peace within those circular walls.

Rather than hierarchy, we need to create authentic circles with our schools. Each circle must have integrity on its own, but still be intertwined with the others. Working together is not a matter of flow charts and lines of responsibility. It involves a new social architecture that must have human striving at the center. We cannot build circular schools everywhere—although more aesthetically pleasing structures would be welcome— but what we need is a social architecture that brings about the harmony one can experience in Olsker and other places on the Earth where extraordinary people have dedicated time and energy to such worthy ideals.

Each school building is surrounded by a larger, invisible structure that is every bit as real as the bricks and wood we commonly see. This larger edifice is made of life forces, the striving of parents, teachers, and staff that serve the children within. The quality of this larger structure is fully dependent on the relationships in and around the school. Each day, parents and teachers either add or detract from this structure, a formative process that shapes the lives of children for years to come.

Thinking, feeling willing, or perception, feeling and will, can be three separate worlds to the detriment of the human being. The need for health is to find the unity, to form a unity out of what has become separate. The round churches are an earthly representation of re-unification. They are an expression of human striving for I–Thou, for harmony, and for constructive "conversation" between humankind and the gods. They stand in humble fashion for all that is complete in human existence and in healthy relationships.

20

The Importance of Administration

As a beginning teacher, I was somewhat oblivious to the administrative side of school life. I entered the school building each morning and all that was on my mind were the children and the lessons I was about to teach. Perhaps this was to be expected for a teacher starting out. If the above pages are burdened by the issues around the so-called veteran teacher and the "sins of commission," then to balance things out one might say that the issues around beginning teachers has more to do with the "sins of omission." And administration was one of them.

Of course it mattered to me who was in the office, and some of the staff became good friends over time. But it took years of work in and around schools to bring home to me the absolutely vital importance of an upbeat, professional, service oriented administration. And as a parent of school age children for almost 30 years, those in administrative roles have come to be a vital link to everything that happens in a school.

Here are a few key aspects in terms of the parent–teacher relationship:

The Front Office and Receptionist

When I was a kindergarten student at the Steiner School on 79th Street in Manhattan many years ago, the first person one met upon entering the building was Blanche Rosse, an elderly woman who had served for many years as the receptionist. She had a one-of-a-kind personality, always willing to exchange the latest news. When a child had a scrape or other small injury, she would administer first aid and top it off with a lollypop. In our sugar-conscious world today, this would no longer be acceptable, but in the 1950s she was often known as Mrs. Lollypop. Most important, she conveyed to parents, teachers, students, and potential friends visiting the building a healthy dose of good cheer and warmheartedness, sometimes a bit of advice thrown in for good measure. Half a century later, that receptionist lives on in my memory.

Now we can fast forward to my son's present school, and once again, upon entering the school one is usually fortunate to find a delightful person at the front desk. She breaks into a ready smile, always has a warm greeting for parents, and is willing to drop whatever she is doing to help. If one wants to get a message through to a teacher, has late paperwork to hand in, or simply needs a copy of a lost newsletter, she is always ready and willing, whether by phone, email or in person. She serves as a vital link between parents and teachers, keeping everything running smoothly.

By contrast, I often have occasion to call schools where I get an unending series of phone prompts and outdated messages such as, "we are on summer vacation and our hours are..." Only, the message is still running in early September. At some schools one never gets a real person anymore, no matter what time of year. There have also been unfortunate experiences of talking with someone only to be interrupted by a teacher or another staff person, and one is put on hold, sometimes without even muting the phone so one can hear internal conversations. And when budgets are cut, it is often the front office person who disappears right away, or has hours reduced to the point that the job is no longer sustainable. I wish schools would realize how many problems are solved and what kind of good will is generated by having the right person at the front desk, answering the phone in person, and serving the needs of parents and teachers.

The Business Manger

Some schools now call this position the Operations Manager, but no matter what the title, this is the go to person for financial transactions. In a world in which so much hangs on money, having the right person in this position can make all the difference for parents, staff, and teachers who need assistance. The qualities I have come to most appreciate at the schools our children have attended are: accuracy, knowledge of each family's particular circumstances, willingness to explain things again and again, as well as objectivity. It is so easy for parents to get emotional about finances, so a school needs a person in the position who is relatively unflappable. The quality of a business manager also has a lot to do with the confidence a board has in the conduct of school administration. Board members are busy volunteers and do not have the time to do financial excavation themselves.

The Development Director

Not-for-profit schools have experimented with this position over the years, and some veer more in the direction of outreach and admissions while others adhere more strictly to fundraising. Especially in smaller schools, it is inevitable that this position always include some elements of community development as well as more traditional tasks such as the annual appeal. The biggest struggle some have had is in staffing this position at non-competitive salaries as well as balancing the issue of required "skill sets" with affinity for the school's culture. Sometimes a school ends up with an IBM type expert who has the skills but offends longstanding parents and teachers with a corporate style, while other situations have a friendly "face to the community" who is at times less than effective in actually raising money. I have become a believer in networking with other nonprofits in the area and sending a development person to professional workshops to acquire the skills necessary. One needs to start with a "people person" who has strong social skills, a background in fundraising (experience with "the ask"), and affinity for the mission of the school. From there, the rest can be learned.

The Administrator

The full time administrator of a school can be the fulcrum of the entire enterprise, or a fifth wheel, depending on the responsibilities and the level of authority invested in the position by the faculty or board. Over the years, schools have evolved this position in a variety of ways, but from the parent–teacher perspective, I feel there are a few crucial ingredients that are timeless:

Confidence. The key word for a position that stands at the crossroad of everything that goes on in a school. If there is confidence, the administrator can act on behalf of the school, take some initiative, and make decisions according to established policies and procedures. If confidence in lacking, the administrator becomes a glorified messenger between the faculty, board, and parents.

Social skills. I have experienced good administrators (our son's school is fortunate to have had one for almost two decades) who are artists at weaving the tapestry of human relations within the school. Ad-ministering is in fact an art form, one that depends both on personal qualities and experience.

Discretion. One has to know what to say and when. There are many ships on the high seas, and navigation has a lot to do with understanding the stars and steering accordingly. Thus at times an administrator has to weave between competing interests of faculty, staff, parents, and board members, looking for common ground and helping people listen to each other.

Follow-through. In the end, tasks must be completed, and the success of any administrator depends on the ability to finish things, despite the many distractions daily.

These are just a few of the key qualities of a successful administrator. There are many more, but when they are exercised, they loop back and generate more confidence, which in turn allows for more initiative and leadership. This is the pathway from management to leadership.

Successful administration is an act of selflessness as described in earlier chapters. If one is truly ad-ministering, one "attends" to the needs of others, facilitating the changes needed without a personal agenda. I have often compared administrative functions to the services provided by a midwife, a vital person who makes wonderful things happen and then moves on. The "baby" in the case of the school is the mission, the new students enrolling, the needs of faculty and parents. Administrators need to be more fully appreciated, understood, and recognized, for without them, much of what happens in a school would grind to a halt. Those that administer in a school are servant leaders in the highest sense.

As Albert Schweitzer said, "Every human being who has the courage to probe deeply into the nature of truth will discover that love which is supreme knowledge."

Family of Origin as Basis
for Social Interactions

Carl Jung described two types of personalities, the extroverted and the introverted:

The extrovert thinks, feels and acts in reference to the object; he displaces his interest from the subject out upon the object, he orientates himself predominantly by what lies outside him. With the introvert, the subject is the starting-point of his orientation and the object is accorded a most secondary, indirect value. This type of man draws back at first in a given situation, as if with an unvoiced 'No,' and only then follows his real reaction.[1]

Jung felt that the introversion or extroversion, as a typical attitude, was an essential bias, which influenced the whole psychic process, habitual reactions, the style of behavior, and the very nature of subjective experience. Our sympathies are connected with extroversion and our antipathies with introversion. Karl König, the father of Camphill Communities, goes on to say:

Our social powers lie in the sphere of emotions. We reach out with our sympathetic forces, and draw back with the antipathetic ones. It is a kind of breathing process, an exhaling in sympathy and an inhaling in antipathy. This is the

---

1   König, *Brothers and Sisters*, 34.

> *human contact-situation. To have very little or no contact at all does not mean to have a great deal of antipathy; it means to have neither likes nor dislikes but a very small amount of emotional ability.*
>
> *It is in the sphere of emotional life and feeling where human beings display their contact with the surrounding world. They meet their environment in the antipathy as well as in sympathy. Love and hatred, extroversion and introversion, are elements necessary as tools for social existence. In childhood we learn to exercise these powers.* [2]

As individuals, we have our particular characteristics: our intelligence, talents, temperament, character. These qualities help make up our personality, which is partly determined by heredity and partly, Steiner would say, a result of pre-earthly experiences. But our social behavior, König and others would say, is largely shaped by our family constellation. It determines how we react to other people, how we make friends or not, how we place ourselves in the community. Even the choice of partners is deeply influenced by the facts of the family constellation. "All these social patterns are guided and formed out by the use of the fundamental forces that establish the relations of people to one another: the powers of contact."[3]

One fundamental way of looking at the family of origin is to trace a person's order of birth. If one is the first or second child born into a family, an only child or a sixth child, one is shaped in fundamental ways that influence later social behavior. These later social interactions, such as parent–teacher relations, are deeply influenced by these early, formative social influences.

If we can become conscious of these childhood tendencies within ourselves and how they influence others we can move from reactive behavior to a more proactive, enlightened approach to these fundamental relationships later in life.

---

2 Ibid., 37.

3 Ibid., 33.

The Only Child

König describes the only child as standing in the doorway—the threshold between the adult world and the world of other children. Such children are observers, reluctant to get involved. Even as part of an activity, they do not fully partake, because they never fully forget themselves. As observers, they maintain a healthy distance between themselves and the world around them.

This ambivalent state in the emotional life becomes so deeply engrained in their whole makeup that they take it with them throughout life. The only child often expects to be socially recognized and valued, because if one cannot be part of many one has to find special standing in one field or another. Later in life they look for an exceptional position in a profession or take up a career path that is distinctive. In social situations later in life, the only child often vacillates between too much and too little social contact because they remain uncertain of their social abilities.[4]

The First Child

In some cultures long ago the first-born child did not even belong to the parents, but was considered the property of the divine being, the leader of the clan or tribe. As a result many first-born children were sacrificed at the altar or exposed to the elements. One could say that the first-born was sent back to the spiritual world to become the protector and guardian of the whole family.

This sets the stage for understanding the first-born as a defender: defender of faith, defender of tradition, and defender of family. The first-born seeks to preserve the past against the onrush of new ideas and trends, i.e., the monarchy in England vs. those who say the tradition is too extravagant. At times the first-born will even feel obliged to stand up for the past whether they like it or not. For this reason, many make excellent judges and lawyers. They seek to uphold law and order, tradition, and continuity. This is partly

---

4   Ibid., 41–42.

because first-borns see themselves as heirs to the throne, with title and leadership of the family. Indeed, for centuries in places such as England the first-born inherited the family estate. This is a privilege but also a burden; much responsibility falls on their shoulders, and from childhood on they will have been trained to be steadfast and responsible.

Yet despite all this responsibility, the first-born are not lonely; they learn to manage other people. They feel accountable for the events around them and tend to take pride in group success. On the negative side, however, they may develop an overbearing attitude to comply with the perceived demands of their position. They might even develop the habit of ordering people around and expect to be consulted before any decision is made. Some can even become bitter and have a sense of deprivation if they do not receove the regard and consideration they feel is their due, considering the tasks that they have accomplished.

Deep down there can also be an undertone of guilt because they have had to forego certain possibilities that were open to others due to taking on premature responsibility. They have had to obey even when they wished to revolt.

Some first-born people are impatient to reach the top of the ladder, not necessarily due to just drive and ambition but also because of idealistic striving and a desire to reform the world. "First children are rarely able to experience the carefree wonder and beauty of childhood. From the start, they are more conscious of everything around them as well as of themselves, and thus they lose the natural attitude of the child. All first children are the piers of the bridge over which others march. This is the special task assigned to first-born children."[5]

The Second Child

In contrast to the above, the second child is often the rebel. Authority and tradition have little claim on him or her, and he/she

---

5   Ibid., 54-55.

will even egg on other siblings against the elder and straight-laced traditions in general. The second child is often the shatterer of conventions, an explorer who loves to discover the unknown. He/she revels in being modern.

König then goes on to compare the first-born to the biblical Cain and the second child as sharing some of the fate of Abel:

Cain is concerned with the transformation of the Earth. Abel's task is to overcome the Earth. Cain is immersed in the tasks of the present; Abel in listening to the past continually tries to prepare the future. Here lies the real meaning of the refusal of Cain's offering and the acceptance of Abel's. Cain's place is the Earth and the smoke of the offering of his fruits and gifts is turned back to the ground whence it rose. Abel's offering is accepted because his place is not the Earth but the Spirit-Land.

> *Abel is rarely a fighter. He is usually a pioneer, a seeker, a dreamer, a poet, and a saint. He is not so concerned with worldly matters. He likes to live without making too much effort. Existence does not only mean sweat and labor; it is joy and bliss, experience and wonder. Abel takes things much easier than Cain. His heart loves the world because it is not such a threat to him as it is to Cain. Abel has a sense of humor and it needs a good amount of disappointment to make him feel embittered, whereas Cain is quickly disturbed and distressed. Cain lives under the spell of duty; life to him is an obligation that has to be honored in every possible way. The Cain in us disapproves of leisure and bliss, of a free day and of a walk through the fields. The rigid laws of the Plymouth Brethren or the Lutherans or the Calvinists are of Cain's making.[6]*

Using an evocative image, König says that being a second child is to walk along a rope stretched between Heaven and Earth, to maintain a balance between above and below.

---

6   Ibid., 62–64.

The Third Child

From defender of the old order to rebel, we now come to the third child who often appears at first as an outsider. No sooner have the first two begun to accept one another and share their lives then suddenly a stranger arrives and makes his or her way into the family. This is a characteristic of the third child: they feel apart or even cut off from other people. However, unlike the only child, which can appear aloof, the loneliness of the third child has a different quality; it can bear the sting of inferiority. At times they can exhibit distrust of other people. They can feel neglected or rejected. When this happens, either they withdraw into themselves and build a wall against the hostile world, or they gather strength and break out of their castle and try to conquer by force what resists them. This force can be physical or spiritual. Thus some of the great saints as well as bold adventurers and soldiers were third children.

To continue the story of Cain and Abel, one can see the redemptive quality of the third child as told in a moving legend:

> *With the third son, Seth, a new story of mankind began. He became the father of all the generations up to Noah who survived the great flood. Cain was the first, Abel the second, and Seth the third. One of the most beautiful of ancient legends tells of Seth of whom nothing more than his name is mentioned in the Bible. The legend tells how Seth, feeling compassion for his old father, Adam, who suffers from a severe illness, goes out to search for the gates of Paradise. He reaches the gate and is granted entry. In Paradise he receives the gift of three seeds taken from the Tree of Life. He bears the precious gift back and when his father dies, Seth buries the seeds under Adam's tongue. Out of Adam's grave a tree begins to grow and out of the wood of the tree the staff of Moses, the pillars of the Solomon's Temple, and at last the Cross of Golgotha were made.*[7]

---

7   Ibid., 87.

So *with the first child we defend the past, with the second we live in the moment, the present, and we prepare the future with the third. The defender of the past tends to be a ruler. The child living in the present is an artist. But the preparer of the future can, in the eyes of contemporaries at least, appear irrational. The only child stands at the threshold of all three, watchful and waiting. All are needed in the web of life.*

So how does this play out in the relationship of parents and teachers?

To begin with, it is important once again to stress the difference between destiny, which is unique to the individual, and the social tendencies, which are nurtured by the birth placement in a family. I emphasize this because there is no law of necessity here—we have freedom on many levels. The freedom that comes with us as our chosen path of destiny, who I am and what I do with my life. And the freedom that comes with my ability to work with social tendencies given through my family of origin. With the latter it is very much a matter of self-awareness. Do I simply act in every situation as a classic first-born, defending the ruling order, or can I see the need to change the status quo and summon my inherent leadership skills to fashion a new order? Or as a second-born, do I instinctively rebel and reject, or can I use my social skills to mend and to heal? Likewise as the third child, when do I need to turn in to deepen my understanding and when am I needed as an enlightened teacher? Can the only child use his observation skills to see what others cannot see and then contribute out of insight? These are all lead questions that come from the need to self-reflect and thus overcome.

This of course is a challenge for every teacher and parent as well. Imagine a first-born teacher who is in a leadership role defending decisions made by the faculty, and in the front row are a group of second-born mothers and fathers who are questioning, challenging, and at times engaging beyond reason. In this situation the teacher and parents could become caricatures of themselves, defender and rebel might engage in a drama that could end up having little to do with the real school issues at hand. Or imagine a second-born teacher at a parent conference passionately trying to reach out to a mother and father who are only children, or perhaps one is an only child and the other a third child. No matter how hard that teacher tries, it will be an uphill climb. My examples could continue for pages, but the reader could certainly pause for a minute to recall instances of such social situations.

What can one do? There is no substitute for the path of understanding. If I can learn to know myself, perhaps I can mitigate and harness my natural tendencies to allow for a better meeting with others. This can be as simple as just "toning it down a bit." Then, if that self-knowledge is met with insight into those I am working with, much good can happen. Teachers can make family of origin discussable, can share their own placement, and ask the family at a conference to share theirs. If it is done out of genuine interest, most will agree to open up (and for those that do not, that is fine—one can still observe!). In addition, if these things are known, one can even context questions and contributions accordingly. For example, when a first-born teacher is explaining the school dress code to two second-born parents, she or he might wish to take a few minutes to describe the faculty process for arriving at the policy and some of the challenging questions and debates within the faculty. The second-born parents will be inwardly relieved that there was debate, and the first-born teacher has gotten off the usual battlements. A few examples or anecdotes can go a long way toward meeting differences. It should be clear that this is not used to manipulate, but to meet the other through greater self-awareness.

An example of an anecdote that reveals an aspect of family placement can be found in the following incident that occurred a few years ago in the field outside our Temple house. We had a spring bonfire under just the right conditions. The wood was relatively dry and the pile was surrounded by the last vestiges of winter snow. All went well. The next day the snow was gone when I went out to inspect, but the embers were still smoldering. On the spur of the moment, I decided it would be fun for Ionas and I to bake some potatoes in the embers. So we stirred them up, buried the potatoes, and went on to play ball while they cooked. A wind came up and blew some of the embers into a patch of dry grass, and I immediately ran back to stomp them out. But the wind picked up even more, and I found myself running around the circle stomping out bits of fire here and there. Ionas, still very young, ran back to the house and returned a few minutes later with a glass of water, meanwhile, my first-born nature kicked in. I was up to this. I would defend our home, and do it single-handedly. I kept running around, stamping on outbursts of fire, until a huge windstorm came up and I knew there was a risk of the fire reaching the nearby woods, which would be a tragedy. So I called the fire department. They arrived in a few minutes and the fire was soon out. Of course I got a citation for this unauthorized second burn day, and Ionas was shaken up. Only when all the drama was over did one of the firefighters say, "You need some attention." It turned out I had serious burns on my face, hands and legs from my solo fight in the field. I had not felt a thing as I had been so absorbed at the time. When Karine returned home a few minutes later she said she saw a troll, not a person, walking toward her across the field with ragged clothes and burns that resulted in a trip to the hospital.

Of course I had been foolish, first in doing anything with the embers on a second day, secondly for exposing Ionas, and thirdly for not giving in sooner and calling for help. Yet I have known other first-born people, and this is a key characteristic: never give up, defend the castle until the end, and pay whatever price is needed in doing so. So I chalk this up to self-knowledge as my repertoire of stories grows with each year of my life.

Self-awareness goes a long way toward humanizing relationships, and family placement is yet another opportunity. As a result of this inner work we can get on with serving the children in our care and the work of the school instead of getting bogged down in interpersonal entanglements.

22

Parent–Teacher Conferences

I f communication and the many other topics covered in this book can be compared to the respiratory system, then with the parent–teacher conferences we come to the heart of the matter. No other interaction is as central to the relationship as the direct dialogue between mothers, fathers, and teachers. In fact, the chapter on survey results near the end of the book will demonstrate that for both parents and teachers, the conference ranked high on the list of vital communication. The most important issues regarding a child's education can flow into this meeting, and if done well, all parties can get to know the child better. It is a golden opportunity for collaboration and the exercise of the parent–teacher partnership.

In this chapter I would like to begin with some of the practical aspects that can help make the conferences a success, and then move on to the nature of conversation. In the inner aspect chapter that follows I will look at something unusual, the "reverse ritual" as a spiritual opportunity.

Practical Tips

Scheduling. With all the stress of our days, care needs to be taken that the appointments for the conferences happen at a time of mutual convenience. This means not just on designated days according to the school calendar, but when all parties can make the meeting without undue hardship. It is far better to have both parents or partners present than it is to meet at 11:00 a.m., when perhaps only one of them can make it. I have a personal aversion to designated "parent-conference days" partly because from the teacher end it makes for a marathon series of sessions that diminish focus and vitality, and partly because it assumes parents can drop everything at work that day, find child care, and hop over to the school whenever there is an empty slot. It is far better to have regular appointments during the school week and even one evening or Saturday morning for those that need it. Teaching is a service, and teachers need to be available when parents can make it.

The Setting. Most conferences are held in the classroom, as that makes for easy access to the student's work and direct exposure to the learning environment. It is ever so helpful when the teacher sets up ahead of time with adult size chairs, student work on hand, and a sign on the door preventing undue interruptions. Likewise, the teacher needs to be dressed appropriately, even if the conference happens on a weekend or an evening. Maryln Applebaum observes "there are some people who do judge people by how they dress...dress for success."[1] If teachers want to be taken seriously, they need to look and act professionally.

Preparation. There is no substitute (even clothing) for this. Rather than just breezing in with an attitude of "lets talk about Johnny," the teacher needs to spend time collecting materials and thoughts ahead of time. This might mean a stack of the child's work, and a note pad with bulleted items to cover. What often receives less attention are the questions you hope to ask and the things you want to find out from the parents. The teacher should collect these thoughts the night before and come fully focused on the child. Parents rejoice when they feel "this teacher really knows my child!" Likewise, parents should prepare their questions and comments ahead of time.

Beginnings and Endings. It is especially important to have a warm welcome to get things off to the right start. Sometimes parents

---

1   Appelbaum, *How to Handle Hard-to-Handle Parents,* 86.

have had traffic or other mishaps along the way, and there is a need to land and find one another before launching into major topics. Likewise, endings need to be attended to, sometimes with a summary, expression of appreciation, or an anecdote that captures the essence of the conversation. Beginning and ending on a strong note gives the conference structure and provides a sense of competence.

Use observable data. This seems cold and scientific, but what is meant is fact rather than subjective statements; both parents and teachers should share what they actually observed. Be as clear and accurate as possible. So rather than say "there have been some social challenges lately," the teacher might say, "yesterday, when the class was coming in from recess, I saw one of the children start pushing which led to . . . " Observations are accessible to all, whereas subjective statements trigger personal reactions.

Make sure all present have ample time to speak. Too often, a conference is a teacher monologue. The meeting then becomes a lost opportunity, as valuable information from the parent side may not be shared, and common picture building cannot occur. By the way, I have also heard parents carry on without letting a teacher say much. A conversation, as will be seen in the next section, involves a coming together of different viewpoints. For that to happen, everyone needs to speak. If one is working with introverts or someone who is just shy, questions can help start the ball rolling. How do you see this? What are you observing at home? How are we doing with homework? Usually one of these will open things up.

Documentation. After the conference is over, take some notes on what has been learned. Both parents and teacher should be clear as to any agreed upon follow-up required. I often put an arrow in the margin of my notes to indicate an action item. Confidence is built when there is timely follow-through.

The Parent–Teacher Conversation

I recently encountered a delightful little book by a Harvard professor who interviewed a half dozen teachers on the nature of the

parent–teacher conversation. Professor Lawrence-Lightfoot intro-
duces the subject as follows:

> To parents, their child is the most important person in their
> lives, the one who arouses their deepest passions and great-
> est vulnerabilities, the one who inspires their fiercest advo-
> cacy and protection. And it is teachers—society's profes-
> sional adults—who are the primary people with whom the
> parents must seek alliance and support in the crucial work
> of child rearing. They must quickly learn to release their
> child and trust that he or she will be well cared for by a
> perfect stranger, whose role as teacher gives her access to the
> most intimate territory, the deepest emotional places. Their
> productive engagement with the teacher is essential for the
> child's learning and growth, and for the parents' peace of
> mind. All of these expectations and fears get loaded on to
> encounters between parents and teachers.
>
> I believe that for parents there is no more dreaded moment,
> no arena where they feel more exposed than at the ritual
> conferences that are typically scheduled twice a year—once
> in the fall and once in the spring—in schools. Although it
> may not be quite as emotionally loaded for teachers, it is also
> the arena in which they feel most uncertain, exposed, and
> defensive, and the place where they feel their competence and
> their professionalism most directly challenged. Beneath the
> polite surface of parent–teacher conferences, then, burns a
> cauldron of fiery feelings made particularly difficult because
> everyone carefully masks them and they seem inappropriate
> for the occasion…
>
> Parent–teacher conferences, then, are crucial events
> because there is so much at stake for the children who cross
> family-school borders, because they arouse so much anxiety
> and passion for the adults, and because they are the small
> stage on which our broader cultural priorities and values
> get played out. In each of these ways, this tiny, twice-yearly
> ritual takes on a huge significance that can be overwhelming
> for the participants.[2]

2   Lawrence-Lightfoot, *The Essential Conversation*, xxii.

Professor Lightfoot then goes on to make a significant point about biographical influences on the participants in a conference conversation, which she calls generational echoes:

> Every time parents and teachers encounter one another in the classroom, their conversations are shaped by their own autobiographical stories and by the broader cultural and historical narratives that inform their identities, their values, and their sense of place in the world. These autobiographical stories—often unconscious replays of childhood experiences in families and in school—are powerful forces in defining the quality and trajectory of parent–teacher dialogues. There is something immediate, reflexive, and regressive, for both parents and teachers, about their encounters with one another, a turning inward and backward, and a sense of primal urgency. The parents come to the meeting, sit facing the teacher in the chairs that their children inhabit each day, and begin to feel the same way they felt when they were students—small and powerless. And when the teachers offer observations and evaluations of their students, they are often using values and frameworks carved out of their own early childhood experiences.[3]

To explore this premise further, I asked my class of soon-to-be teachers at Antioch University New England to write a couple of pages on a childhood experience that has influenced their present attitudes toward teaching or parenting. They submitted some insightful material, a sample of which is included in the appendices. What came from this exercise is that each person has in fact significant childhood experiences that still hold sway in present-day consciousness.

Student Ana Reiselman's paper on the subject is a particularly striking example.

> I was nervous. The classroom was unfamiliar and bare, with only desks and a piano. The other girls and I clutched at

---

3   Ibid., 3–4.

our music and ourselves, hearts beating quickly with desire to be the chosen one. Ms. Francis, our seventh-grade chorus teacher, sat on her bench, ready to play. The song was "Shenendoah," and we all wanted to sing the opening solo.

I was used to being overlooked at this point, but that didn't make it any easier. I had so much passion and feeling for music, and I couldn't figure out why nobody was able to recognize what felt so obvious and clear to me. When I was seven years old, I had memorized *Les Miserables,* the musical, in its entirety, and could and would sing the whole thing on day trips throughout New England as my parents and I gazed at the beautiful foliage. I was brought to tears in the backseat of the car as I suffered with Eponine and Jean Valjean the many injustices and heartaches the world had brought to them.

Waiting my turn, I sat in my chair and listened to the other girls sing. They all had beautiful voices, every one of them different. I had spent the last year and a half watching them get cast in leading roles and given solos. I felt that my voice was not quite as good, but I was fairly certain I did have something that they did not: a space inside of me for the music to live the way it wanted to live. A place where the song could whisper, "This is me—please show the world. Show me as I am, not as you want me to be."

Ms. Francis signaled to me that it was my turn to sing. I could feel myself shaking as I walked up to the piano and stood next to her. Closing my eyes, I silently said hello once more to the song, and asked her to reveal herself to me, so that the world may hear her as she wished to be heard. My teacher played the opening chords, and I began to sing... "Oh, Shenandoah, I long to hear you. Away, you rolling river. Oh Shenandoah, I long to hear you. Away, we're bound away, cross the wide Missouri..." The room had fallen silent, a different kind of silent than when the others were singing. I felt an acute listening, as everyone, myself included, felt the presence of something that couldn't be named or seen. Ms. Francis stopped playing, and thanked me. I was the last to audition, and we all gathered our things and left, uncharacteristically quiet and solemn.

The next day at chorus rehearsal, we waited as usual for the daily announcements following warm-ups. I sat fourth row back, fifth seat from the aisle in the soprano section. Mrs. Francis stood up from the piano and said, "I know I usually take a longer time to announce who I've chosen for the solos, but I would like to start adding her in as soon as possible. Ana, could you please stand and begin 'Shenandoah' for us." The room began to swim in front of my eyes, as I slowly stood to sing. I looked into my heart for the song again, and asked for her to help me.

As human beings, we have an innate drive to expand ourselves and become more, while at the same time harbor a deep need to truly be seen by one another. I believe that the teacher's role is to see the human being in front of them, as Ms. Francis saw me. Since that day, all of my favorite teachers have been the ones that took the time to really see me and my gifts, drawing me forth into the world so that I might better share what I had to offer. I have so much gratitude that my teacher, despite having a hundred students in her seventh-grade chorus alone, took the time to really look. It was her looking that changed my life, and gave me the confidence I needed to step more fully into my role as a giver of stories, a role that I have continued to play for twenty years.

From this place of truly seeing, we must as teachers strive to ask the right questions; the questions that when answered by the student will open up new and beautiful vistas inside of them. When this incredible act occurs, both the teacher and student stand in a new doorway together, each seeing something completely and wonderfully different. Within this spacious trust of togetherness while developing individuality, education can go anywhere."[4]

I found these responses to be a full validation of all that Dr. Lawrence-Lightfoot has contributed to the theme:

4   Ana Reiselman, paper for "Evolving Consciousness," 2013.

The adults come together prepared to focus on the present and the future of the child, but instead they feel themselves drawn back in their own pasts, visited by the ghosts of their parents, grandparents, siblings, and former teachers, haunted by ancient childhood dramas. These visitations and echoes reverberate through the room, complicating the conversation and filling the spaces with the voices of people who are not there, people who are often long gone.[5]

These voices from the past, so to speak, play into the conversation between parents and teachers. It is sometimes like a theater in which the actors wear masks, the presenting "selves" which often obscure the biographical "selves." Yet there is an inner dialogue going on all the time, an internal conversation within each parent and teacher that may have painful memories, cultural and ethnic influences, stories of success and abuse, frustrations and unresolved emotions. There is a vast sea of drama under the surface of the parent–teacher conversation.

These generational echoes are double-edges for both parents and teachers. They are a source of guidance and distraction, insight and bias. They sometimes lead to important breakthroughs and discoveries in the conversation, and at other times force an abrupt breakdown and impasse. But for the most part, these meta-messages remain hidden, inaudible, unarticulated. They are the raw, unvarnished subtext to the ritualized, polite, public text of the conversation. They are the unconscious, diffuse backdrops to the precise words that fill the foreground dialogue.[6]

Thus we need to realize the dimensions of this phenomena and its potential influence. Deep-seated attitudes are brought into the conversation, some of which may barely be visible. How do we work with this? Indirectly at best. One cannot go fishing for personal, confidential material, and there are realms that are beyond the rightful scope of a school conversation. But every once in a

---

5 Lawrence-Lightfoot, *The Essential Conversation*, 3–4.

6 Ibid., 5.

while one person will open the window a bit to reveal something that might hint at a biographical influence. When that happens, rather than try to analyze (these are not therapy sessions) one can perhaps share an anecdote from one's own childhood. These shared moments bring people closer together, and over time, become part of the growing knowledge base of human relationships. One always has to treat these matters with extreme tact and delicacy, but one can observe, remember, and increase a sense of sensitivity when one has been allowed to get a glimpse of influences from the past. Once gleaned, these insights need to be guarded with the utmost confidentiality (not shared at a staff meeting) and held in a respectful place close to the heart.

23

Parent–Teacher Conferences as Reverse Ritual

In cultures around the world people celebrate in the form of rituals, from tribal customs in Africa, to Native American ceremonies in what is now the United States. These rituals were used to draw a community together in shared practices, and remind the participants of their connection to their common spiritual traditions. Churches, synagogues, and mosques around the world also rely heavily on ritual. One could say that many of these rites and rituals serve as an invocation, inviting the descent of spirit into matter. They call down to Earth spiritual content that serves to energize and unite a community.

Rudolf Steiner describes the above as one way to build community, one that has deep historical roots. He then also describes another route, something he names as a reverse ritual, in which human beings become so active with one another that spiritual content is generated and sent in the reverse direction, from the earth to the heavens. How can this happen?

In lectures on Community building given in February 1923, Steiner describes three stages of consciousness: dreams, which occur without much personal direction, waking consciousness that arises as we interact with nature and daily life, and then a third level which is particularly interesting: "We begin to develop the first understanding of the spiritual world when we awake to the spirit and soul of the other person."[1] *When we work spiritually together, with reverence and dedication to the common idealism, we do not have a ritual descending so to speak into our midst but a community spirit that ascends. "The individual persons awake to one another, and they awake to each other in a changed condition each time that they gather together, as each of them in the meantime has gone through a different experience and advanced somewhat further."*[2] *If one works time and again together to create spiritual substance, and one awakens again and again to the others, one finds the spirit at work on the Earth and enacts a reversed ritual. One could say an offering of human striving results in an entirely new substance woven from human working out of Anthroposophy.*

When a teacher in a Waldorf school meets in conference with the same parents again and again, sometimes three times a year over eight years, a substance is created that might be called a reversed ritual. A tapestry of connected conversations, dedicated to the best interests of the child in question, is gradually woven over time. Especially if the participants are spiritually active, it is possible to feel a change in the atmosphere of the conference over time. One does not have to begin at the beginning each time, but there is a continuity that supports and strengthens the work. One cannot say much more about this phenomenon, for it is ever so delicate. But I encourage those who participate in these conversations over time to observe what happens, and at least entertain the possibility that something is being offered up that is greater than the words spoken in any given conference.

Behold, I make everything new.

---

1   Steiner, "Community Building, p. 11.

2   Ibid.

24

The Uber-volunteer

Every nonprofit I have known relies on volunteers, and independent schools are no exception. A Waldorf school is often fortunate to have parents serving as class reps, chaperons on field trips, costume and stagehands for dramatic productions, workers at the fundraisers such as the holiday faire, and a host of other events throughout the year. As is so often stated, the tuition charged only covers a portion of the costs of running the school. The rest is made up through the annual appeal and volunteer labor. The hope is that through these extraordinary efforts the school is able to open its doors to a more diverse population of students, and that a variety of scholarships is available. Without volunteers, all this could not happen.

As I wrote at the end of my book *Initiative,* volunteering is not just about the school, but also about community and self-development. We grow as human beings when we volunteer. A community thrives when many participants serve out of love for the task without financial consideration. I have served again and again, and some of my best friendships have grown out of the part of my life I call community service.

Managing volunteers is a task unto itself. One cannot just accept any offer that comes through the door, and one has to be sure to coordinate efforts. Some schools even have a volunteer coordinator; others use their existing administrative staff to carry out this function. However it is done, there are a few essentials in working with volunteers:

Screening. A school is a professional organization, and one cannot have just anyone dealing with finances, for example. Especially board positions such as Treasurer, but also committee members and other volunteers need to be screened to determine if their skill sets match the task. Some schools feel awkward doing this, but if it is neglected, dysfunction, chaos, and disillusionment can set in.

Supervision. It is so easy to say, "Now we have that task covered, we can relax." But in fact, just as in any workplace, supervision is needed. But who has the time to do that, and when there are problems, does anyone have the courage to address them with a volunteer?

Evaluation. When a task is completed, there needs to be an evaluation, not just to give feedback to the volunteer but especially for the sake of the school so that next time the task can be refined or one can make a better selection of people to work in that area.

Generally schools are very reluctant to "manage" volunteers because they are devoting so much time to the school and no one wants to appear ungrateful. But if management does not occur at least in the minimal way described above, the paid administrative staff can actually inherit more work in constantly "cleaning up" after volunteers. And the volunteers themselves can become frustrated with the school as a whole if their experiences are not positive.

There are four areas that need special attention in regard to volunteer-heavy nonprofit orgainizations:

Leadership selection: one need clear criteria, a process for selection, and clarity as to decision makers, to name but a few. A school or other nonprofit cannot afford to just "accept" whoever is willing or nominated for a leadership role such as board president. There is too much at stake.

Boards, PTOs and other volunteer groups within a school need to attend to continuity and succession. I have known boards that have a sudden turnover and all institutional memory is lost, not to mention valuable expertise. The role of vice-president should be more that a formality, as this person ideally spends a year of two getting ready.

In organizations that have limited resources we sometimes find that a poverty mentality sets in: "we are lucky to have anyone....." kind of thinking. Yet having the wrong people on the board can further diminish financial resources, while raising volunteer standards can increase them. Even a small school needs to attend to professional standards and act as it was already a large school.

Crisis management is often a true litmus test of a volunteer-rich organization. How will the school navigate in rough waters? Has the school developed resilience or not? A crisis tests our leadership metal (see chapter in *Organizational Integrity*).

Finally, there is a phenomenon I would like to call the *Uber-volunteer,* those who, year after year, go beyond the norm in volunteering for tasks. This kind of person can appear to be a literal gold mine, as they not only serve countless hours, but because they get to know the school so well, they need less supervision and can be relied on to finish tasks in an appropriate way. These folks often show up at the pioneering stage of the school, some emerge later as class reps and then move on to chair the holiday faire, others serve many years on the board and various committees. I have known some who practically live at the school! One might think that this super-volunteer is a gift from Heaven and all one can do is wish for more such people. Yes, of course that is true, but I have made some observations of these folks, and have a few cautionary notes to sound.

Often these wonderful people are frustrated in their own professional careers and the school becomes a vehicle to serve while in-between jobs. This is not in itself a bad thing, but I have observed that under the hours and hours of volunteer service, one can detect a level of personal dissatisfaction professionally, which, if not addressed eventually, can become corrosive. One can observe a one-sidedness to these peoples' lives, in which the school becomes the be-all and end-all of life. One has to guard against a lack of balance in which the super-volunteer loses perspective and "becomes" the school. I have known a few who continue slaving away for the school long after their children have graduated. Do they have a life?

If something goes wrong, let's say the school experiences a crisis, the super-volunteer is affected in a major way. It is hard to stay objective when one's identity is so closely bound up with the school. For example, if the school has a budget deficit, the super volunteer who served as chair of annual giving or the fall harvest festival might feel personally responsible, just as one does for one's own family budget. Things can get subjective very quickly with a super-volunteer, especially since they do not have the natural correctives and balancing that teachers get from each other and the children.

How does one transition out of an Uber-volunteer role? It is not easy, for giving up any aspect of the many tasks can be seen as a defeat, or simply as letting people down. More often than not, I have observed that the super-volunteer leaves in a major huff, and has to "write off" the school 100% in order to regain personal balance or restart a career.

I feel a school has a responsibility to work with these extraordinary people and not just let them take on more and more. It can become downright unhealthy otherwise, even a kind of exploitation. The faculty leadership or the administrator can seek out the super-volunteer and suggest redirection toward training new volunteers or a diminishing of roles for a time for the sake of building up more group responsibility. One should be able to have "sabbaticals" for volunteers in which the person can take some time off before a re-entry. There are many strategies that can be used, but I urge schools to consider the human resource issues involved in volunteerism more seriously.

Volunteers are a resource that is not inexhaustible, and just like any natural resource for which we are grateful; we need to attend to sustainability, both for the individuals concerned and the healthy functioning of the school as a whole.

25

Beyond

The other night I reconnected with my friends, the stars, not the ones in Hollywood but the ones up in the night sky. I quickly found the Big Dipper and started looking for other constellations when I suddenly decided to stop that and just look. So I adjusted my position and looked again.

It was still early in the evening, so I saw a few very bright stars beckoning in the night sky. Then as my eyes adjusted I saw a few others that were very faint; they were there as very small specks of light. Then I had an overwhelming feeling that there were many, many more stars up there that I was not seeing. The heavens above were filled with stars and I was only seeing a few of them! I felt very small standing on that grassy field with such a majestic dome above me.

Afterward, when back in the car, I reflected on how so many things in life are right in front of our noses, sometimes literally a few inches away as with computer screens and iPads. Then there are things nearby but less visible, such as the voice of a friend on the phone or a child looking out of the window of a school bus. But perhaps life itself is populated mostly by things we do not see. And I decided that I needed to make the case for living life with the ever-present reality of the invisible.

In fact, spirit comes before matter with things that matter most. Inspiration precedes a poem, a design lives in the imagination of *the architect before it appears on the drafting table, and my words live in me before they appear on the screen. One can go on and on with this list of spirit before matter, and usually one comes back to life changing happenings such as love before children, music before composition, hurt before tears. The really important things that happen in life usually begin in the invisible, spirit realm before they manifest in the material world around us.*

Advertising would have us believe otherwise. The materialism around us wants us to focus just on things, implying that if we have more of them we will be happier. Many people get on the conveyer belt of material acquisition and it becomes a kind of conquest, until a crisis or life change forces them to reevaluate.

The same is true for education and the attitudes we bring to bear on schools. Do we evaluate success based on tests, performance, and "outcomes" only? Are we in fact comfortable saying that a good education needs to be measured by criteria that demonstrate immediate results? If we fall into that trap we forfeit most of what is good about learning, namely the growth of ideas, skills, and capacities over time. The real "outcomes" of education cannot be seen until 10, 20, 30, or more years later. Yet no one seems to have the patience or understanding for the long-term perspective.

I often use the analogy of my orchard. Imagine planting an apple tree and then measuring its "success" after one year. No fruit? Cut it down, for it was a "failing apple tree." Or if given a year's reprieve as being a "troubled apple tree under watch," would one measure it again, and if again there was no fruit, then surely one must cut it down? The trees I planted in my orchard 10 years ago are only now bearing ample fruit, and I am content, knowing that given some care (and not too many New Hampshire blizzards) they may continue to do so for my children and their children. This is the story of growth.

Education needs to get back into the mode of learning for growth and human development, and out of the business of factory production. We need to lift our gazes out of our test scores, which in my life have proven meaningless anyway, and back to the wider picture. We need to look at the horizon, not the pebbles.

When parents and teachers come together to support schools for their children, they need to examine their values and expectations. If a teacher is planting an orchard and a parent wants widgets from the factory or vice versa, we have a problem. As school communities, we need to discuss our intentions. There are, and should be, a wide variety of schools available to parents. Choices need to be made. But for the relationship of parents and teachers to work, there needs to be an alignment of expectations and attitudes toward education. These things need to be discussible; otherwise there will be constant disagreements on the particulars.

This does not mean that an orchard orientation should neglect the "here and now" aspects of education. One needs tools, and basic ingredients, for growth. But can we also straighten our backs after planting and see the horizon, or do we stay in the realm of the earthworms?

Parents and teachers need to share their expectations for education to see if there is common ground for working together in a particular school. For instance, in a Waldorf school, there is often a common understanding that life embraces both the visible/known and the invisible/unknown. Children instinctively know more about these things than meets the eye, but what about the adults around them? Are we willing to search for what we cannot see?

> *I feel an unknown force that ripens,*
> *Which gaining strength, grants me myself;*
> *I sense the seed maturing*
> *And boding light-filled weaving*
> *Within me for my selfhood's power.*[1]

---

1   Steiner, *Calendar of the Soul*, verse 21.

26

Parent Evenings, Class Nights

It is a tradition going way back in educational history to have evenings at the school when parents come in to experience what their children have been doing. These events occurred in the well-known Laura Ingalls Wilder stories of the one-room schoolhouse, and in our larger consolidated public schools today. Parents enjoy sitting in the child's place, seeing the work that has been accomplished, and listening to the teacher talk about the curriculum. Here are some of the highlights I have experienced over the years:

The stories of how the children are dealing with the material can be entertaining, funny and ever so informative.

It is great to experience the curriculum first hand by doing various activities such as drawing, math through motion, singing, and geography. One gets to know the personality and style of the teacher much better when one experiences a real lesson in the actual classroom similar to the one that their child experiences each day.

It is fun to work with other parents on a project, or have a lively conversation on a current theme. One discovers that one is not alone in facing certain struggles, and sharing stories helps provide support and encouragement. So for example, one might ask, "What do you remember from seventh grade? What was it like being 12 or 13 years old?" This brings out a sense of common understanding and purpose in the parent–teacher group.

Some teachers are highly directive during a parent evening, planning, leading activities and doing most of the talking. I remember one class night years ago when the teacher went on for over an hour and most of the parents were tired from a long day at work. Several of us struggled to stay awake. In contrast others see themselves more as facilitators. They plan a few key questions and then encourage a discussion among parents. I have found that just as one modulates the curriculum around child development, so it is best to vary the methods used over time. In the early years of an eight year "Waldorf journey" it might be helpful to be highly directive, as the parents need to know the "what and how." But if that remains the style for too long, parents can disengage, or even stop attending. The teacher needs to continue to bring in activities, but as the years go by put more focus on group conversation.

By middle school the class teacher might actually have some of the parents leading segments of the meeting. This could include a conversation on such topics as planned field trips, sex education, or guidelines for home use of technology. Much can be achieved when parents talk with one another without the constant filter of a teacher. Nonetheless, as long as the event happens at school, the teacher needs to "hover," listening actively and jumping in when needed. The faculty is responsible for every event in the school.

Some parent evenings are well attended and others are not. It is particularly hard to get both parents or partners when there are still younger children at home. One might want to vary the night of the week and even the time somewhat to be more inclusive, as well as occasionally asking some older students at the school to provide babysitting in a neighboring classroom. A teacher also needs to work hard at getting attendance from both moms and dads, for if that does not happen, or at least if they do not alternate sometimes, family decisions on educational matters can be skewed by uneven information and experiences. To this end, it is also better to have a well-attended parent evening than to have a long one. As a long-time parent, more than 90 minutes becomes a burden. Those who go on longer usually do so because of poor facilitation or lack of adequate planning, both of which reflect poorly on those responsible.

Throughout this book, the primary theme is the threefold aspect of human capacities, and once again this can be considered in regard to parent evenings.

Thinking: A good class night should have significant conceptual content. This might include such aspects of child development as curriculum, school projects, and academic goals for the year. However, we also need to challenge the parents' thinking by considering the *why* and *how* and by raising contemporary issues in education such using computers for homework. Most teachers tend to give too much weight to the "thinking" aspect of the class night, trying to "tell" parents what is happening in the classroom through their natural enthusiasm for the work. But this can result in parent passivity unless they are also engaged on other levels.

Feeling: This realm is often most directly activated through conversation. Parents want to discuss how their children are doing and the social life of the class. A major contemporary theme is bullying and teasing, which can occur on a variety of levels. Through the work of Kim John Payne and those who have completed his training, there is now considerable expertise available to schools on these social issues, but parents want to share perspectives and experiences. Every class night should have a facilitated conversation, not just questions and answers to the teacher. Another way to engage the feeling aspect of parents is through artistic work such as singing, painting, and movement, all of which engage parents beyond conceptual thinking.

Willing: This segment of the meeting involves *doing*. Parents enjoy working on something that has engaged their children, such as making a geometric drawing, doing math, or modeling a pyramid. This aspect of the meeting need not involve much talking, but can be extraordinarily healing for those who have had hectic days and want to enter into the world of ten-year-olds. After doing a project, it is good to take a few minutes to reflect on the experience, thus looping back to the conceptual and emotional aspects again. Ideally parents will emerge from such an evening refreshed and recommitted to the school.

Just as a true education is holistic, a parent evening should engage the whole human being.

My survey of parents included a question on what makes for a successful parent meeting or class night. Here are a few sample responses. Others can be found in the appendices.

"A good parent meeting has an organized agenda (the number one request from the parent surveys), with attention to time management, and with child care provided by older students."

"A teacher who is not afraid to control the aggressive parents who sometimes take over making sure that their children get the same special treatment that they get at home."

"Needed: agenda, good facilitation, good process, ending on time."

"Having it on a weekend...weeknights are too difficult with bedtime/dinner and family activities."

"Full turnout of parents. Sharing of pedagogy, some sharing of anecdotes and a limited amount of business planning."

"Like anything in life, everyone wants to be heard and appreciated. There are many topics that can and should be broached as the years progress—some are simple yet important; some are controversial and will never be resolved. Regardless, the teacher's ability to hold a group of parents through the various discussions that occur during a class meeting in an open dialogue and respectful space is key to a successful meeting...and even a successful group of parents. It is unfortunate but in this day and age our teachers need training in this area just as they need training on how to be teachers. If a teacher can work even half as well with the adults as they do with the students, the chances for a successful class with minimal attrition are high."

"Openness and honesty. Remembering that parents have different parenting styles and that one family's way of being is not necessarily the same as another's."

"Personally, I do not want the entire meeting to be about how much help the teacher needs and all about signing up for every event of the year. I want more info about what is going on in the classroom..."

"Humor and lack of anthroposophic dogma!"

"Organization, an agenda and timeliness."

"Less lecturing and more information as to what the children are doing. It is extremely difficult to get to these meetings so having them less frequently and more in depth is important to me."

"The teachers must realize they are speaking to adults at this time and treat them as such."

"Starting on time and as many parents attending as possible....keeping the business to a minimum and leaving time for parent–teacher discussion about topical subjects."

Parents mention again and again the importance of an agenda, facilitation and timeliness for parent meetings, and yet these topics never came up in the teacher responses. Perhaps one has to sit in a small chair for a couple of hours to understand the parent perspective!

Finally, if we want to have good attendance, we need to work with both mothers and fathers. Thus the following chapter will focus on this theme, not just in terms of parent evenings, but also in regard to the entire parent–teacher relationship.

27

Mothers and Fathers

In this chapter I will explore the parent–teacher relationship further by looking at how each parent may have different needs and how administrators and teachers might work with them.

In an interview with a seasoned administrator, I asked about working with mothers and fathers in the context of school. She began with the preface that of course there are moms that act more like dads, and dads that act like moms, but that in her experience the differences are greatest at the early childhood level. Because of the physical connection young children have had with their mothers pre-birth and into the early years, mothers tend to be tied in with their child's first steps at school in many ways. So this administrator said, that the first day of school, for instance, needs to be smooth and wonderful for both the child and the parent.

For a mother, issues such as the comfort and emotional support of the homesick child are paramount. These things are also important for a father, though they may express it differently by asking, for example, if all the outside doors can be locked.

In the grade school, this administrator wishes she could guarantee every parent that their child would be accepted at a college of their choice, for that would alleviate many anxieties. If the dads in particular are confident in the academic progress of their child they will relax and go with the flow, even accepting strange phrases such as "thinking with the heart." What helps moms enroll their children and keep them enrolled is any talk about the features the school offers—movement classes, foreign languages, or remedial help when needed. For fathers, this administrator added that it is important to talk about the benefits, such as how two recess periods each day help the children focus better in the classroom.

Dr. Lawrence-Lightfoot addresses this issue even more directly:

> "Moms and dads come at this in a different way."
> "How so?" I ask, intrigued by both her statement and her caution in making this bold observation. "Moms are patient, and dads are impatient with the children and the dialogue about the children," she responds immediately. "And often dads express a jealousy and envy for the moms' knowledge of and intimacy with the child that gets articulated in the conference."[1]

Because fathers tend to spend less time at their children's school, they are often less familiar with the social relationships in the class-room. For instance, as a dad, it takes me longer to even get to know the names of the other children. But there is also the issue, raised by Lawrence-Lightfoot earlier, of dads' own childhood experiences, which can well up in what he calls the "doorknob phenomena," as they find themselves back in a school setting:

> The parent–teacher conference is over; the father rises to leave and heads for the door. He touches the doorknob, then turns back abruptly with one final thought that he delivers passion-ately. "And another thing," he blurts out, referring to a topic that was covered earlier in the meeting. "That same thing happened to me in fifth grade, and I swear it is not going to happen to my child!" His tone is threatening; his teeth are bared. His anguished outburst surprises even him. His pas-sion explodes in defense of his child and in self-defense of the child he was.[2]

This can also be the case in a more benign way as well:

---

1   Lawrence-Lightfoot, *The Essential Conversation*, p. 56
2   Ibid., p. 3.

Paul Holland, a top executive in a major technology firm and the token African American to occupy such a lofty position in his company, sends his two children to North Star, an elite, "progressive" private school in Seattle, Washington. He is on the school's board of directors and—along with his wife—is deeply committed to being a "visible presence" in the school and a "fierce advocate" for his children. When he comes to the parent–teacher conference for his son, Stephen, a third grader, he is filled with "an undeniable terror" that he may hear "bad news" (even though Stephen's school reports and classroom assignments have shown steady improvement) and a "particular bias" (that teachers do not recognize his son's potential and have not challenged him nearly enough). Like, Paul, Stephen is a whiz in math (with an "aptitude in the stratosphere"), and yet Paul feels that his teacher has never really pushed him to achieve or celebrated his gifts. Paul's meetings with the teacher are marked by his steady insistence that his son is capable of achieving more and his urgent request that his teacher set higher standards and challenge him to meet them.[3]

The danger of characterizing mother and father responses to conferences, call nights and school interactions in general is that they can easily appear stereotyped, even old fashioned at times. Yet if one actually takes the time to listen to what mothers and fathers say in interviews, as I did for this book, there are some things that come through in a more traditional way. I feel it is important to hear what fathers and mothers are actually saying, rather than right away filtering everything through our own lenses. That is why I supplemented my interviews with an extensive survey (see survey results in chapter 32).

Here is a perspective from one mother:

Mothers seek to guard a child's soul: is he/she loved, cared for, fostered, held. Mothers are very interested in their child's social standing in the class, and how classmates deal with

---

3   Ibid., p. 24.

social issues when they come up. A mother cares deeply that her child comes through the school experience "intact," not obscured by dumb teaching or insensitive classmates. "I don't care so much about his/her score in basketball but more whether my child's true being can shine forth. Is my child "seen" and recognized by others?

This mother continues in regard to fathers:

Of course a father also cares about his child's soul, but it shows itself in different ways. A father wants to know if his child will make it in the world, be able to function as a productive member of the community. Will my son or daughter fit in? Standing on a basketball team is an indicator of this. Fathers want to raise sons and daughters that are "real," productive and successful by outer as well as inner standards.

When I surveyed teachers about whether there is any difference in their interactions with mothers or fathers, 17 out of 42 said "no." Some of those who said no seemed to equivocate a bit with other descriptors that indicate a wish to say there was no difference but were not sure.

Male teachers reported that they have sometimes had to be more careful in dealing with Moms as they can be more "volatile," "overprotective" or blind to their child's challenges. Reference was made to "tiger moms." None of the male teachers reported problems relating to dads.

Female teachers reported they also noticed a difference in dealing with moms on an emotional level that they "read into things more than fathers" and can show more emotion. One added, "With moms I can be more tender."

All teachers agreed that moms are more involved than dads, especially in the lower grades. Fathers are seen by all as less emotional, less involved, more interested in their child's academic progress rather than the child's emotional wellbeing.

Male teachers seem to have more difficulty relating to moms than female teachers do with dads. Yet only female teachers report more "tension" when dealing with dads. Since everyone seems to see dads as helpful but less present, schools need to look for ways to get them involved!

The parents were asked in the survey: Is there a difference in terms of relating to your children's teacher(s) if one is a mother or father (if the parent is a mother or father)?

Their responses were so extensive and so varied that the reader will need to look in the appendices for that question. This is obviously an important issue that many have felt, experienced, and lived, yet have up to now had little space for discussion in school settings. I urge all concerned to take this up as a conversation topic (see, for example, "Why on Earth?" in the appendices).

Just as we work with learning differences in the classroom, parents come to the school with different backgrounds and attitudes. A wise teacher or administrator is willing to inquire, listen, and learn so that these expectations and attitudes can be met. In my experience many things that later develop into issues had an origin in lack of attention to differences, attitudes, and expectations. When the gap between these and the reality of the experience grows too great, tension and even conflict can emerge. As with issues of physical health, a bit of prevention, in this case proactive relationship building early on, can go a long way.

28

Spiritual Streams

*A*nyone glancing at the cover of this book will see the words "parent" and "teacher," which may imply a duality. Yet only in the most simplistic ways can the notion of polarity enter into the picture, because as soon as one begins to work with the between, the relationship, a third element enters in. And in looking back on the previous chapters, especially those in italics that indicate the inner path, the notion of threefolding comes up again and again. Almost every topic considered urges us to move from the "two" to the "three," from polarity to active engagement. This is once again the case with the following section, which will attempt to describe spiritual streams and how they influence our vocation, attitudes, and ways of interacting.

On his deathbed, the Dutch therapist and consultant Bernard Lievegoed described three spiritual streams that are present especially in those who are working out of Anthroposophy. His thoughts were published after his death, with a forward by Christopher Schaefer, under the title, The Battle for the Soul *for those who wish to read a more complete account of his thoughts. What follows is a brief characterization of the three aspects:*

The Path of Knowledge

Those who most strongly work out of this impulse seek to understand the world through insight and the acquisition of knowledge, *both conventional and spiritual. Building on the work of Aristotle and others, Rudolf Steiner (himself very much part of the path of knowledge) spoke in the Foundation Stone Meditation: "For the Spirit's universal thoughts hold sway/In the Beings of all worlds, craving Light."*[1]

The spirit is in the reality and craves for release, for the light. The task of human beings is to humanize matter, to win freedom of thought. The Michael School, founded by Steiner, is a new form of university where various fields of learning (education, science, arts, medicine, and so on) are researched in light of spiritual science. One could say it is an anthroposophic university. This is the direct outcome of the Erkenntnis path, the way of knowing.

People who find themselves in this group are thus often in the field of education, training centers, nonprofits that offer workshops, retreats, and programs for professional development. What they have in common is a commitment to learning, as learning brings insight, which in turn can help us understand and then solve the issues of humanity today.

A person in this stream, when faced with a challenge might want to first read a book on the subject, Google the topic, or do a literature review. These folks want to understand the dimensions of the issue before being called upon to act.

The Path of Doing.

This stream is very much connected to the great initiate Christian Rosenkreutz, whose presence has been experienced on the Earth many times over the last centuries. Earlier associated with alchemy, the people in this stream are intent on transformation, on working with earthly realities and bringing about change. They want to act in and with the world, doing practical things that make a difference. Over time, through these efforts, the Earth can be made into a work of art, ennobled.

---

1   Lievegoed, *The Battle for the Soul*, p. 37.

I witnessed a wonderful example of this in August 2013 when observing a two hour process of glass blowing at the Baltic Sea Glass Co. in Bornholm. Beginning with a small chunk of material, a red-hot furnace, and a series of long blow rods, the husband and wife team worked for two hours creating one incredibly large glass plate. The audience observed in rapt attention for two hours! Here, before my eyes, was a Rosicrucian master at work!

Those in this stream are quite at home in the arts, but can also be found in farming, medicine, pharmaceutical work and other related fields. These folks are patient; they know that good things take time such as glass blowing and a farm is not converted to biodynamics overnight. Those in this stream are willing to use a developmental approach to issues, and see metamorphosis at work.

The Path of Healing

This stream rests in-between the other two and is one that is often overlooked, for these folks work quietly, often behind the scenes. If Rudolf Steiner is seen as a preeminent example of the Erkenntnis (knowledge) stream and Christian Rosenkreutz of the path of transformation through doing, then Manu can be taken as a spiritual guide of this third stream. Through his teachings we know that every light creates darkness, and something good creates shadows. But the shadow of the good must be treated with gentleness; we must develop gentleness toward evil (what a novel concept!). Manu taught that gentleness and love can save the human soul, and then we will be better able to help humanity. Indeed, the Manichaean principle is "one of the pillars of social work,"[2] for the soul is the battlefield between good and evil. The spirit is unassailable, so the battle has to be fought on the soul level.

Those in this stream want to help people who are unhappy, challenged, abused. Here we find the whole field of therapy, psychology, hospice, physiotherapists, organizational consultants and others who work out of an impulse to heal. A friend of mine works in a

---

2   Ibid., 88.

clinic for veterans, and his stories are straight out of this spiritual stream. Lievegoed adds: "An important group is formed by parents, who give a number of years of their lives to their children."[3]

Those in this work are process oriented, and they are often extremely selfless. They put the patient/client first, and try to work out of attentiveness and the present moment to affect healing. There is also a degree of humility in that they know in the end, the patient/client has to do the work themselves, and the therapist becomes less and less of a factor in the process. They step back as the healing progresses.

So here we have again three different approaches to life! The first seeks to know, the second to act, and the third wants to heal. Now if we put this into the parent–teacher equation, what a difference it makes where a parent or teacher is coming from. A parent who is a therapist may have a very different way of working than one who is a college professor. Or a teacher who is working developmentally out of the Rosicrucian stream may mistake a parent's simple request for more information/knowledge on an issue. As with any spiritual matter, it is important not to "peg" anyone, as in fact we all have some of each of the streams in us, but awareness of these different approaches can help us treat one another more gently, with greater care, and with a growing interest in "who are you?" The perspective of spiritual streams can inform us in the art of relating.

A note: People also change over time. During the first third of my life, I worked mostly out of the path of knowledge, seeking degrees, teaching, and landing a job as professor. In the next period of life I was still on the knowledge path, but what really got me going in the morning was doing—*establishing organizations, development programs, serving on community boards, gardening, and doing things in a practical way. Now, as I enter another phase, what draws me out of the future is the path of healing, which can be served in a*

---

3   Ibid., 93.

variety of ways, some of which are still unknown to me. If I can go through phases, perhaps those around me are also changing over time—yet another call to open the heart.

> *In constant self-creating,*
> *Soul-being becomes self-aware;*
> *The cosmic Spirit forward strides*
> *Through self-cognition new enlivened*
> *And shapes from darkness of the soul*
> *Will-fruit of sense of self.*[4]

---

4   Steiner, *Calendar of the Soul*, verse 24.

29

Waldorphans

One topic that has received little attention in the literature on Waldorf education concerns the particular placement of teachers' children in the mix of school life. Although few would want to admit it, they can represent a group unto themselves, both in terms of common characteristics and challenges.

The positive aspect of teachers' children is that they have many opportunities to experience the full life of the school, from festivals to play rehearsals, setting up classrooms to end-of-year cleanup. They learn to be helpful, both to their parent–teacher and to others, from office staff to teachers in need of an extra pair of hands. Rather than spending time in day care, they can often be found in a classroom after school doing a drawing or something creative while the parent is in a meeting. They know everyone, and can come to feel like the school is a second home.

The negative aspects include long hours at the school, irregular schedules and a feeling that their parents have forgotten them when meetings run overtime. They often seem to drift around the school, almost begging to go home with a friend, and they can inadvertently become privy to personnel matters that tinge their relationship to other teachers. Sometimes there is a vague aura of neglect around them—thus the term Waldorphans.

Yet where things get really interesting is the relationship of a teacher/parent to other teachers, in particular the ones who teach the child in question. A teacher's child is often the subject of informal communications in the hallway, and behavior issues are telegraphed within minutes. I remember one colleague who finally said to another. "I refuse to talk about my daughter with you during the school day. Please make an appointment and my husband and I will have a parent conference with you." This was understandable, yet it should not have to go that far. The teachers themselves should set the boundaries around the parent–teacher relationship. (Please see the section on teachers' children in the chapter Survey Results.)

Over the years I have found that this boundary setting needs to involve several considerations:

There needs to be agreement between teachers who educate each other's children that when they discuss the child, they are in a parent–teacher relationship with the customary protocols, and when they are in a faculty/staff meeting or otherwise doing school business, they are colleagues. Phrases such as "I am wearing my parent hat..." can help.

If there is a father or mother who is not part of the teaching staff that person should always be included in communications and conferences. It adds objectivity.

When there is a dispute, the teacher with a child in question or the teacher teaching that child can call upon the school administrator or faculty leadership. I remember one case in which the teacher wanted the child to be put back a year and the parents, including the teacher/parent strongly disagreed. The issue split the faculty, as some took sides on the merits of the case and others around perceptions that due process had not been followed.

There needs to be a system of mediation that is invoked sooner than might otherwise be the case, as a dispute among colleagues of this nature can send a strong negative signal to other parents if it is not resolved quickly.

A school also needs to set up protocol around recusal, as there are some decisions that affect a family in a way that the teacher/parent of a particular child should not be seen as influencing. The ones that have been most difficult occur when normal disciplinary practices are amended or lightened for a teacher's child. As one discouraged faculty member once said to me, "We were worried we would loose the whole family." Translation—the decision about the child would have resulted in a respected teacher leaving the school.

I feel teacher's children should be enrolled in the afterschool program when they stay late, and should follow all the customary expectations for families that enroll their children, including dismissal time.

A teacher's child with special needs presents yet another layer of challenges to the school. Does the school have the resources to deal with the needs, and if not, how are communications handled. And if the school does have the resources, is there special billing to the family of the teacher's child? How are reports handled and what happens if inadequate progress is made? These are but a few of the issues that need to be addressed in these cases.

A child of a teacher employed at the same school has an unusually complex relationship to the school. If handled well, those children can become leaders in the upper grades due to their special understanding and their relationships to other classes and many teachers. If neglected, they can fall between the "cracks" and become Waldorphans. I suggest each school open up a conversation, at least within the faculty, about how they intend to meet the needs of teachers' children. Even if this is just a beginning, it will raise consciousness around a long-neglected issue. Surely we want to serve the needs of all the children in our care?

30

Inclusion

Many years ago, when I was Faculty Chair of the Great Barrington Rudolf Steiner School in western Massachusetts, I had the honor of interviewing René Querido, a leading figure in the Waldorf movement and a founding member of Rudolf Steiner College in Fair Oaks, California. At the time, the school was trying to improve the parent–teacher relationships, and so I asked him for advice. He shared a picture of inclusion that has stayed with me ever since. René said that a healthy Waldorf school should be willing to include at last three different groups of parents:

> One group could be characterized as those that simply want their children to be happy, safe and surrounded by a good learning environment. They identify the school as providing these things, and they are then content to drop off the kids in the morning and let the school do its thing. These parents may come to important school events, especially those that involve their children, but otherwise they are not active in the affairs of the school. These parents may be fully booked professionally, or they simply have confidence that the teachers know what they are doing and parents should not interfere. The parents from this group want simple, clear communications that do not require much deciphering. They can become annoyed if the school expects too much volunteering, and would prefer to give to the annual appeal rather than spend hours on a committee. They feel that the school

should charge what is needed in tuition, and let parents otherwise run their own lives. If their children are happy, they are happy, and these parents do not inquire much about the curriculum or the philosophy behind it. That is a matter for the teachers to handle.

A second group could be called parent activists. They show up for almost every event at the school, volunteer for field trips, committees, and almost always agree to help even at considerable personal sacrifice. These folks do want to know about the curriculum because that is what affects their children on a daily basis, but the philosophy behind the teaching may remain vague concepts. These activist parents tell you what they think, have regular interactions with administration, and can be relied upon to come to class nights and assemblies. When schools refer to "the parents" it is often with this group in mind.

A third group, according to Rene, is a group that may not only be active, but also demonstrate special interest in Anthroposophy and the foundations of the school's mission and vision of the human being. These folks will not only go to assemblies and volunteer when possible, but they are especially keen on parent–teacher study groups, workshops, guest lectures and foundation studies such as those provided by organizations like The Center for Anthroposophy. They do it not just out of dedication to the school but also out of growing personal interest in human development, meditation, and the evolution of consciousness. Some of these parents over time sign up for Waldorf teacher training and may even return to their school as teachers later on. They want in-depth communications from the school that includes the philosophical aspects, even in the newsletter and emails. They yearn for depth.

René then went on to say that challenges arise when a school assumes communication with just one of the groups and neglects the others. So for instance, if group number two is the mindset of the faculty, then groups one and three will feel overlooked. The members of Group 1 may drift away, and parents in Group 3 may cause problems because they feel their questions on Anthroposophy are not being met, that the teachers are being secretive, and that the school has something to hide. These parents can become especially challenging because they already know something about what "should be happening" in a Waldorf school, and are quick to point out the indications from Rudolf Steiner on why one needs to provide such subjects as eurythmy and two foreign languages.

The three groups have different needs in terms of emails, regular letters, and the news bulletin. Group 1 wants to know what is happening and when. Group 2 wants news of the classes, experiential sharing of life at the school, and progress reports on the building and fund raising. Group 3 wants all of the above plus in-depth coverage of the curriculum and Anthroposophy. Slanting the communications just to Group 1 may make the school seem much like any other school run by professional administrators. A Group-2 slant can make Group 1 feel guilty for not participating more, and a Group-3 slant can make the others feel they have been signed up for an indoctrination program. And these aspects pertain also to verbal communications between parents, teachers, and staff. But with a little insight into which group one is speaking with, it is not too hard to calibrate answers to meet the needs of the person asking. Here is an example:

Question: What is Michalemas?

Answer for parents in Group 1: Michaelmas is a school festival we celebrate on the last Saturday of September in which the children perform the legend of Michael and the dragon. We also have games and refreshments, followed by a school cleanup. The event begins at 10:00 a.m. and ends at 1:00 p.m. All school families are welcome.

Answer for parents in Group 2: Michaelmas is a school festival…it is part of the curriculum as both the story of St. George and the higher counterpart we call Michael. The drama the children will perform depicts the classic battle of good vs. evil and becomes part of the character education of a Waldorf student. The cleanup afterward is not only important for the appearance of the school, but it is also good for the children to see parents and teachers working together.

Answer for parent in Group 3: Michaelmas is a school festival. As you know from Anthroposophy, in a Waldorf school we work with the development of capacities, including thinking, feeling, and willing. Steiner often spoke of Michaelmas as a festival of the human will, forged through concrete deeds on this Earth. When you watch the drama and participate in the cleanup, you will be enacting this aspect of human striving in what is really a very new festival on this Earth.

The wonderful thing about this approach is that parents are left entirely free to be who they are or migrate from one group to another. For instance, the progression from group one to two and then three happens quite often, and teachers need to keep an open attitude toward changes in a parent's orientation. But it is also possible that a parent gets a new job, has a spell of really demanding assignments at work, and moves from group two to group one. Schools need to be accepting of this sort of thing, and parents need to be articulate in expressing where they are, not only in terms of the life cycle issues, but also in their ability to participate, volunteer, and so on. One cannot be sure of where any one parent rests within the groupings mentioned by Rene, but one can at least have a faculty/staff discussion of how to differentiate between parent needs and how best to communicate with them.

In fact, one of the main purposes of this book is to encourage parents and teachers to rely less on assumptions but instead develop greater insight and confidence out of which to share where they are in any given school year. A healthy relationship requires forthright, clear communication based upon growing self-awareness. We are mutually responsible for the social fabric of a school.

Now a few words about inclusion as it pertains to faculty and staff. There are at times issues, some of them taboo, which affect the healthy functioning of a school. When they occur among the faculty and staff of a school that also claims to be a community, they can sap the vitality of the entire organism. Parents are for the most part unaware of the issues that follow, and many are not even deemed discussable within the faculty.

Silencing. A young teacher was hired by a school and given a mentor. In one of their early meetings the mentor said that it was school policy that a new teacher not speak at faculty meetings for the first year. So the new teacher acted accordingly, and unless asked a direct question, did not say a word in those meetings the entire year. When the school year was over, the faculty did a review, and one person turned to the new teacher and said, "We missed your voice in our meetings. We hope you will share more in the future, as the few times you spoke we really appreciated it." The new teacher responded by sharing what the mentor had instructed, and the mentor put her hand in front of her mouth and said "oops." A whole year had gone by without the new teacher feeling part of the faculty conversations; this was an issue of inclusion, owing to false assumptions and a lack of commonly held group expectations.

I feel this type of thing happens when the school is not clear on common expectations of new faculty and when there is insufficient orientation. Faculty, staff, and parents need orientation to school policies, where to go with questions, and what to do when certain things come up. The case study above arose, in my view, because the mentor teacher was left alone to cope as she saw fit. But we cannot govern our schools by singular personalities, a theme that has sounded throughout this book. We need to move from the level of personality to objective truth and transparent policies. The age of the old fiefdoms is past; the age of the consciousness soul has arrived.

Power and Control. These are words most often used in terms of politics or the military, but they can at times be reality in a school. There are those that seem to exercise more authority, and even after some years at a school, there are often teachers and staff members whose voices seem to count less. If this is the case, it needs to be brought out into the open for everyone to consider. The classic case that I often hear about is when a meeting takes up an issue, say the program for the graduation, and certain things are decided. Everyone goes home that night thinking they know what the program will be. Then the program comes out and it is different. If one dares ask, the answer might be, "Oh, it went back to the such and such committee and this is what was decided." I have learned to have a healthy suspicion for the phrase "it was decided." The "it" more often than not is not a committee but a person who talked to a few others outside the meeting and had the program changed. This is a matter of power and control.

Human resource (HR) issues. In the not-too-distant future I would like to convene a workshop on HR training so that faculty and staff can learn some of the basics about personnel decisions. For some of the decisions that come out of a faculty/staff meeting, as reported in newsletters and in interviews, are downright illegal. There is the case of a female applicant for a job in a Waldorf school who was asked in her interview, "So, what are your plans for having children? We are concerned that you might not stay with the job." In another case, a pregnant teacher was told she had to leave work at such and such a time due to her pregnancy. Another prospective teacher was asked to change out of her khaki slacks before entering the room for a job interview. These instances put an entire school at risk. All schools need to follow best HR practices and legal requirements in terms of hiring, firing, and other personnel matters.

Undermining. This is a more subtle issue, as often even the victims do not know at first what is happening. But when people are undermined and disempowered, they are not able to participate fully and it becomes an issue of inclusion. Although many examples can be given, in this instance I would like to highlight the importance of language. Sometimes our words have far more impact than we imagine. After a report, the chair might be heard to say, "Now, for a more complete picture of the situation...." Implication: the previous report was not complete, and the person who gave it is left feeling inadequate. Another way of undermining is when someone makes a suggestion and then is totally ignored. One is left wondering, "Where do I stand?"

Emotional blackmail. Whenever one works in groups, there is always the potential for emotions to run high when the issues are contentious. What is not often so easy for a new teacher is to see how the expression of strong feelings can be used by some to win an argument. Storming out of the room, raising the voice and other techniques can produce shock and disengagement, which then leaves the field open for a few to work their will on others.

Zealous advocates. There are times when a person or small group will take up a cause, such as building a new early childhood building, starting a remedial program, or beginning a high school, and commandeer every conversation, every agenda, every resource available until they get their way. These efforts often leave a bitter taste in many mouths, and the lack of inclusion in the process ultimately undermines the success of the very project they were so zealous about in the first place.

Bringing up some of these issues may in themselves be controversial, but I find that if any of these situations arise (and I have named just a few of the more frequent ones) it is best to name them and ask the group to discuss what is happening. One may have some justification to fear falling victim to the same phenomena mentioned above when one brings up a difficult issue, but in the end, it is better for the school if there is a clearing. I have found that often the best way to raise the topic is by asking a question, such as "Are we all okay with the level of inclusion on this issue? Or, have we all had a chance to speak and be heard with respect?" The other benefit of bringing it up as a question is that sometimes one perceives incorrectly, or incompletely, and having a discussion can clear things up. But it is always better, in my view, to engage rather than to marginalize. Once patterns get established in a school, it is much harder to bring about changes. When too much time goes by, one often needs outside help whereas if one catches things early on, a system can self-correct.

When in doubt, ask a question and help make things discussable. Groups can bring about correction when given a chance.

Before leaving the topic of inclusion, I would like to add a few thoughts on diversity. Some independent schools have a diverse student population and work actively with a multicultural education. Others still have a long way to go. Some of the challenges relate to finances (inadequate scholarship money) and others can be based more upon geography and the ethnicity of the community in which the school is placed. But no matter what the challenges, it is essential that all schools strive for a curriculum and teaching methods that value multiculturalism as a matter of good education, not just about who is in the classroom. One of the few conditions Rudolf Steiner gave when asked to open the first Waldorf school was that it be open to all students. They established a tuition free method of support (a private association provided the funding) and everyone, not just the children of the Waldorf factory, were admitted. In those days, it was even unusual to have both boys and girls in the same room, with all children participating in all subjects. Having traveled to Nepal, India, Australia, Norway, Africa, Canada, and many other countries in which there are Waldorf schools, I feel that the Waldorf movement is truly diverse on a global scale. Where further work still needs to be done is in terms of local situations and especially teaching methods and materials. As some of our more famous graduates, such as Kenneth Chenault (head of American Express), assume leadership roles, I hope that soon we can establish more extensive training for teachers and adequate scholarship funds, perhaps through AWSNA, to allow for further progress in terms of inclusion.

And parents and teachers can join together to become ever more articulate advocates for our shared ideals. This should be part of the conscious goals of a school, and needs to be renewed each year at all school retreats so everyone remembers what we stand for. Too many things suffer from benign neglect. We need rituals, events, retreats, and group gatherings that remind us why we are all part of our school.

31

An Extension of Consciousness

*L*iving in town most of the year now, we are able to walk or bike
to many stores, cafés, or restaurants. So it was that one day
recently Ionas and I found ourselves walking down Main Street,
then turning right onto a side street in the direction of a shoe store.
We talked about shoes, the choices, makes, and his needs. It struck
me that my consciousness was filled almost exclusively with the
notion of "shoes." After a successful purchase, we made our way
home and both moved on to other things.

This level of consciousness, which for clarity's sake I will here-
after refer to as "shoe consciousness," is one that we employ regularly. It is functional, practical, and centered on the here-and-now
of living. Without it we would soon cease to function and would
need others to care for us. It is characteristic of Anthroposophy that
there is a healthy respect for this shoe consciousness, in that it keeps
us grounded and citizens of this Earth.

To go a step further, let me ask the reader to imagine another
walk. This time I am on a familiar nature trail, and after drinking
in some of the beauty around me, my thoughts turn to the administrator of our local Waldorf school. I find myself thinking about
her role, what it might be like to interface with so many people in
a day, and what her challenges and life questions might be at this
time in her life. My consciousness is now living with "the other,"
which is a higher level than the shoe consciousness described earlier.

Even though there is no material goal in sight, such as a purchase or planned meeting, my consciousness allows me to be somewhere else. Almost coincidentally, I have often found that when I think of a community member like this, I often end up bumping into them later in the day!

Now for a third stage, imagine that I am not the only person thinking about the school on that particular day, but that in fact the school is facing a question, and parents and teachers have been asked to weigh in. It might be an expansion, new program, or scholarship fund. In any case, now on that given day, we have several dozen people thinking about the school. What happens? Since thoughts are realities, it is as if a life force is extended in the direction of the school, surrounding the school with light-filled consciousness. This is a very important aspect of community building, and can be used to do many good things for a school or organization when it is taken seriously.

In the field of research there is a value called the Heisenberg principle, which affirms that the subject of research changes when attention is focused on it. This can present a challenge to those who strive for complete control of the research process, but for a living organism such as a school it is a great benefit. A school can change for the better when parents and teachers take up a common question or vision!

Teachers have long used this when they do "the child study" in Waldorf schools. Through a structured series of observations and discussions, teachers try to understand one of their students better. By pooling their observations and insights, they learn more than any individual teacher could discover alone. Frequently, however, when a challenging student is taken up in this way, changes begin to occur, even during the process. Within days, teachers often report improvements in the child's behavior or academic work. When attention is devoted to anything living, it is affected.

This has tremendous implications for parent–teacher work in a school community. Rather than just focusing on the here and now tasks (shoes) of running a school, leadership is needed in providing leading questions and themes for the collective attention of the group. When this happens, new ideas come forth, people step forward to help who had not been involved before, and resources become available. Extended consciousness leads to increased vitality for the entire school.

Of course, there are often struggles as well, and sometimes one needs a crisis to awaken extended consciousness. When something troubling is happening, then people also rally around, sometimes in a critical way. But even those challenges are a form of consciousness-raising.

There are times in the life of a school when parents and teachers have to suffer each other, struggle fiercely in order for something new to be born. Suffering and birthing seem to come together often as part of the package.

32

Survey Results

As I began to write portions of this book, I realized how important it would be to listen to what parents and teachers are currently saying about their working relationship. It has been many years since I was an elementary school teacher and some might think I was now out of touch with today's teachers. Likewise, although I have been a parent for many years, some readers might speculate that my views have been unduly influenced by the half dozen schools my children have attended. But even more important, from a pure research point of view, I thought it would be good to vary my sources: books that are included in the bibliography, my experiences and observations of the many schools I have visited, and a survey that could take a wide sweep of parent–teacher responses. For this "triangulation" to occur (using three or more methods of qualitative research) it would likewise be important to attend to best practices in conducting surveys.

Thus I began with a draft of two surveys, one for parents and one for teachers to fill out. I showed it to a couple of colleagues for a first read, made a few changes, and then did a test with some alums and people I met at a summer conference. By the end of the summer I was ready to go, but a colleague at Antioch kindly reminded me of the IRB requirements (internal review board) that had been established since my last comprehensive survey done for *School Renewal* many years ago. So I submitted the survey for review with the proper authorization forms, introduction, and so on. The reviewer made some necessary and helpful suggestions (which I took to be requirements), I made the changes, and I received permission to go ahead with my project.

Knowing the limitations of time for all concerned I decided not to survey the universe, but selected five Waldorf schools, two on the east coast, one in the Midwest, one in the Rockies, and one on the west coast. Two of the schools were K-12, the other three K-8. One school decided to only distribute it to teachers, which was okay with me as I knew there were fewer teachers than parents in the population group. Some responded by filling out a hard copy, but many did so online using a special web site my daughter-in-law created for me. In the end, I received 56 responses from teachers and 241 from parents.

Overall, there were many answers that I could have expected, but there were also some real surprises. I have referred to the survey a few times in other chapters, and some responses are also in the appendices, but in the pages that follow I would like to share a few of the results, both for the sake of those that stand out and so as to give the reader a flavor of current parent–teacher thinking on these issues.

Parent Survey: What are the greatest challenges you have faced as a parent working with a teacher? Out of a total of 241 responses, 45 respondents had not experienced challenges, and were very happy with their teachers. Some responses addressed multiple issues, and were each entered in the multiple categories they belonged to. Not all responses addressed the question, and were not included. The most frequently mentioned issues were:

1. Communication (C 1) as in the "act of transmitting information." The ability to "hear the other"—to listen, to make people feel included.

2. Communication (C 2) as in the means of communication. Including timeliness, responsiveness. Effective means of getting the information to the other.
3. Boundary issues. Parents feeling excluded from their child's classroom life. Parent not able to find a way to help.
4. Time issues. Parent finding the teacher too busy/over-worked. Parent too busy.
5. Personal conflict. Criticisms based on the teacher's personality traits.
6a. Child related problems. Parents feeling that the teacher does not understand their child. Academic progress issues. Fair treatment.
6b. Concerns around children with special needs.
7. Trust related.
8. Lifestyle. Criticism on parenting. Alternative families.

It appears that communication is at the top for both parents and female teachers, followed by child related conflict and personal issues. Lifestyle issues are a much bigger challenge for the teachers than for the parents.

Teacher Survey: What are the greatest challenges in working with parents?

The challenges of teachers again involve communications and issues concerning a child (22 Responses).

Communication becomes an issue when the direct line between teacher and parent is broken, and the issue travels outside of this line to other parents: "gossip and accusations;" "parents who go to someone else about an issue with you"; "parents form a lobby group to oust a teacher."

The second aspect of communication that causes frustration is information sent home not being read, parent evenings not attended: "Parents not reading letters or losing information;" "When I feel I repeat myself over and over . . . making announcements at meetings, write the same announcements in a class handbook and in email form and still some parents miss the information." "Don't come to parent evenings, yet bring me their issues."

Teachers expressed difficulties meeting the parents successfully with issues concerning their child: "overprotective parents;" "helicopter parents." "Helicopter parents rob their children of credit for success and responsibility for failure."

This theme of teacher's frustration with a parents' lack of ability to see the larger picture when it concerns their child as a member of a group, was expressed several times: "single minded focus on only their child without regards for the greater needs;" "Hard to see for some parents that their child is not simply the victim in a situation" (in which altercations between children occur). "Food issues, when parents want the whole group to adjust to the needs of one." "The belief that every resource in the school be given to the child regardless of the effect of that child's behavior on the class." "Parents who show poor judgment with the class or favor their own child."

Difficulties were mentioned also communicating with the parents about a child with special needs: "In early years of our school (and even now too) when our resources were so much less, and a child arrives who needs more than the school is capable of providing...there's the rub." "We feel unable to meet the needs of a child (staff or resources) with learning or social challenges, and parents cannot accept that."

Support and Understanding of the Education

Teachers expressed challenges when parents are not actively participating and supporting their child's education:

"Parents who simply do not support the discipline measures at school;" "unwillingness to support the pedagogical recommendations or take the necessary steps for change;" "Parents who show no interest in the 'why' of the education;" "not understanding the curriculum and because of it, complications occur either for their child, for them, or for both." "unreasonable expectations."

Lifestyle Issues

There was no mention of this response from male teachers. Female teachers expressed problems concerning the compatibility of life at home and life at school: Parents who are in denial about how something they are doing is negatively affecting a child...such as poor diet, late bedtimes, being habitually late, too many activities; home-styles not being aligned with Waldorf values; too much age-inappropriate material and treating the child as an adult. When parents are inconsistent with their discipline at home, it can make classroom management more challenging.

Boundaries

This is the story about power and control, about listening to the other, and about bullying. When parents take a larger role in the life of the school or in the class than is comfortable for the teachers, problems can arise. Comments on this include:

"Parents who insist on being a larger presence in the class than is wanted or needed"

"When I was a new teacher, the parents seemed to feel the need to take charge."

"Parents who are board members try to take over parent meetings."

"Finding the balance between having parents help, while maintaining enough control over things such as car riding assignments."

Issues of close friendships with parents were also mentioned, which can blur professional boundaries. Surprisingly, issues of trust between teachers and parents were rarely expressed explicitly or clearly as the main issue in a conflict. This plays a role, of course, in other issues already covered.

An interesting aspect of the parent–teacher relationship has to do with children of other teachers in the school. Question: Do you have a teacher's child in your class and, if so, what advice can you offer when working with the parents of those children? Only one respondent did not feel there was a difference or a problem in dealing with children of colleagues in the school.

Working with the children of colleagues was seen as "delicate," "more difficult," "sensitive," "tricky," "difficult," or "not easy!" Advice echoed the sensitive nature of this work: "tread more gently," "give forewarning when the child is discussed," and "think four times before saying something."

There were suggestions to wear the teacher or colleague hat consciously and to be explicit about which role you are assuming before speaking with a parent-colleague. This was mentioned six times by female teachers and not at all by the male teachers.

Advice: remember that these colleagues are "parents first, and then teachers." Do not assume a normally supportive colleague is also a supportive parent.

Advice: bear them in mind as you plan events. Try to include them. Understand if they cannot participate.

What makes you pay attention to suggestions from parents? Do you listen to some parents more than others? Why?

Out of 56 responses, 15 respondents (2 male and 13 female) feel that they treat the parents equally or strive to. Otherwise, teachers reported they listen more to parents with these qualities:

- are informed about the education
- are objective, reasonable, and realistic
- have a feeling for the class as a whole
- are open
- are respectful toward the teacher
- have expertise or experience in a particular area

Some also reported that they see their work with the parents as a partnership or as teamwork.

The most telling number story is that most teachers pay attention to suggestions from some parents more than to suggestions from others.

In regard to suggestions from parents, here is a sample from the parent survey on the question:

12. *What do parents need from a teacher in order to feel met and supported?*

"Transparency of the teacher's teaching and classroom management. Parents need to know that challenges and conflicts are being addressed and that a resolution does not exist until the teacher and the parent believe it does." "Clear, relatively frequent communication. Occasional communication and feedback on your particular child, not just the class as a whole (this is probably more of an issue for parents of children who do not have any particular learning or behavior/social issues). Invite the parents on occasion to see what the class is doing all day or tell them about it. Opportunities for parents to participate or volunteer if they are able, but no pressure for working parents." "Honest communication and non-judgmental listening. I want to hear where my child needs support and improvement, not just what a shiny star she is. Waldorf teachers have a wealth of information that can help me in my parenting and I want to learn it. Raising a child is not always sweetness and light. How do we handle the tough times?"

"Parents need to understand the curriculum. Teachers need to have awareness and be sensitive to spiritual/religious orientations. Open communication channel (comfort and ease with communicating openly)." "Communication; I need to feel heard. I am paying several thousand a year! I want to be heard. I think that more social opportunities might help." "Quick responses to questions that are clear and not emotionally charged." "Acknowledgement that parents are/have been heard." "Compassion; to be heard, teacher can repeat what you are saying."

"Reassurance that their child is doing well and finding the way, and that their child sees." "Communication, communication, communication, and transparency—especially around challenging times and issues." "I firmly believe that a happy, excited, and growing child and class is what parents need most. Secondary is to be kept in the loop about what is happening in the classroom and parent expectations so parents can plan accordingly."

"Openness to parent questions and involvement. Working together to overcome learning difficulties, especially when outside help is needed. Strong ability to present the curriculum so that parents feel confident about what is happening in the classroom. The only time I've had a difficulty is when a teacher had a closed-door classroom policy and was unwilling to discuss what was happening in school." "Not just listening, but hearing." "Open to listening to parent concerns with empathic disposition." "Interaction with us. Acknowledge us when they see you. Small talk is a place to start. Emails are good."

"Updates on child's progress in school." "Just to feel that they are being heard and to be educated on what we don't understand, which in my experience Waldorf teachers do an amazing job at."

"Knowing that the teacher actually knows your child, is aware of his or her struggles (as well as the families struggles) and communicates frequently about problems…and successes [I would love to hear more of that on a more frequent basis]. Regular, short emails help to make parents feel secure in what is going on at school and provides a perspective that can ward off problems when a child tells a 'crazy' story about what a teacher did. The most amazing stories can be told about the simplest incident. A child can easily make the teacher look unfair or unresponsive. More communication is better."

"Absence of defensiveness. Openness to parent's plight. Coming from a place other than fear. True wholeheartedness. Willingness/ability to be vulnerable. Plus, truly feeling they have been heard and understood. And acceptance that a parent's gut/intuition is usually worth listening to."

"To feel supported by the teacher I think it is important to have a timely response to emails. That is my preferred form of communication with direct questions with simple answers. If I required a meeting it would be nice to have that obliged in a timely manner."

"Availability and approachability. Knowing that a teacher is available for evening phone calls or after school meetings without it seeming like a hassle is important. Parents know teachers are overworked and underpaid—we don't like to impose. But a teacher who makes it clear (in words and deeds) that they are available for questions and conversation makes parents feel much more met and supported."

"Parents need to feel that teachers care, that they see and can articulate issues, that they have reflected on a plan to deal with issues and that their concerns and comments come from a sound understanding of the relevant issues. Authenticity is also very important."

"Precise, detailed examples of a problem their child is working through, how they are struggling and how they are being supported. Best delivered via parent–teacher conferences. This gives the parent confidence that their child is understood and being cared for or "held" as they grow and learn."

"Recognition." "Openness to the parent's perspective and a willingness to listen and hear the parent's concerns." "Understanding and communication." "Clear, prompt, transparent communication. Timely support for social or academic challenges at school. To be welcome in the classroom. To have clear expectations around homework. Respect for parenting choices and use of strong, kind guidance for suggesting parenting techniques that work with the Waldorf curriculum."

"Regular communication. Quick response to email and phone calls. Follow through on proposed actions." "Engaged, willing to listen and follow up on concerns individually or with the class as appropriate." "Good communication skills with the parents and students alike."

"To feel understood (loved and respected). To feel that the teacher really cares about their child. Also, some parents need to know that the teacher is there to teach and that they need to trust the teacher to teach (so somehow the teacher needs to demonstrate competence). To experience the teacher as knowing more than the parent, not in arrogance, but in a "here is something that can help explain what is going on" sort of way. And conversely to acknowledge that the parent knows their child and has info that would help the teacher."

"1) A listening and compassionate heart. 2) Secure and mature emotional health. 3) Never taking a tone of defensiveness. 4) To always look for solutions, not blame. 5) To guard the confidential information of all at all times. 6) A bright and quick sense of humor. 7) The demonstration of deep care/affection for the students."

"Again, I think respect and acceptance of differences. Communication and a sense that we are all on the same team." "I think this depends on each family, each family is unique. In my case, it is purely knowing that my kid is in the best and warmest hands each day. That she is being held. This is so reassuring to me. Really feel blessed."

"A sense that our child is being met. This sense is built by their progress and development. Whenever something out of the normal range happens, we need communication." A sense of competence, professionalism, warmheartedness. "A real sense that the teacher knows their child. Understands how best to serve them. That emails are read and phone calls returned right away (even if it is just to say, 'I received your message and will get back as soon as possible')."

"Clear honest communication." "Feedback on their child—positive and negative." "Two-way communication. A sense of being welcome in the classroom (within reason)." "A willingness to hear the parent, discuss as necessary and work together to find a solution (if one is necessary). Also teachers need to come forward when there is a long standing issue with a child in the classroom, rather than leave it alone and hope it goes away." "Effective listener and compassionate heart."

"Honesty even when it's uncomfortable. Clear expectations communicated to all. A clear picture of what's going on in the classroom socially as well as academically. Requests for input/help from the teacher vs. feeling closed off from the day-to-day. Creative partnering for developing solutions to problems and to enrich the curriculum or relationships." "Communication."

☙

Early in the survey I asked both parents and teachers for their preferences in terms of methods of communication: telephone calls, hard copy letters, emails, class nights, parent–teacher conferences other. Doing some analysis of the results, I found: Parents and teachers were in almost complete agreement that phone calls are very helpful, ranking them first or second in a majority of cases. They were also in alignment in terms of the value of parent–teacher conferences, ranking them very high in terms of successful communication.

Things got even more interesting in finding significant divergence in some of the other categories: By a 6:1 margin, more teachers thought sending letters home was more important than parents did. By a 2:1 margin, parents felt emails were very helpful. And by a 4:1 margin, teachers felt class or parent nights were more helpful than did parents.

☙

This raises interesting questions. Given how much time teachers spend preparing parent nights and writing letters home, has anyone told them that though appreciated, these are not seen by parents as the most helpful modes of communication. Now granted, there are other reasons to send home letters and do parent nights, such as the need to share curriculum and develop a fuller picture of how a group of children handles their developmental changes. However, if we place communication as one of the most essential goals of a successful parent–teacher relationship, then surely teachers need to consider what parents need most, which includes emails, telephone calls, and parent conferences. Given limited time and energy, it would seem that teachers need to devote more time to conferences, phone calls and emails, and parents need to advocate for what works in the relationship.

There are many more findings in the appendices, but the survey served a vital purpose; it established once again the importance of our working more intentionally on the parent–teacher relationship. This is a matter of urgent importance for our schools and for our leaders.

Those in positions of authority need to take note. For instance, in a wonderful document prepared by the Pedagogical Section of North America called "The Core Principles of Waldorf Education" (see appendices), seven key principles are stated. Only one has to do with relationships in general (#6) and even there one finds only minor reference to the subject of this book: "Relationships. The task of the teacher is to work with the developing individuality of each student and with the class as a whole. Healthy working relationships with parents and colleagues are also essential to the wellbeing of the class community and the school."

We need to move the parent–teacher relationship from the "are also" category at the end of priorities to the top of the list. It was not for nothing that Rudolf Steiner, when asked, "How many children can we have in a class" answered: "How many parents can you work with?"

How many parents can we work with as a school movement? Perhaps our enrollment at AWSNA-certified schools is an accurate answer to that question. Some schools seem better able to work with the parent–teacher relationship than others are. Perhaps it is time to say "we all" value and recognize the fact that we cannot succeed without the partnership of parents and teachers. We need to model a relationship that our children will seek to emulate.

33

The Door

During a course I teach each summer on Research, I ask the students in the Waldorf Teacher Education Program at Antioch University New England to find a parable to share with the class. Rather than reaching into biblical traditions, they are encouraged to find an object in nature or in the classroom and describe it in detail. As a second step, they are asked to "lift some meaning" from the object to show a wider perspective, a spiritual essence. They do this in short, two- to three-minute presentations, and it serves as an early teaching moment in which the class and I can then give constructive feedback.

Recently one of my students used the doorway into the classroom as her parable. She described the physical door in detail, and then ended by mentioning that they, as students, are different when they enter and when they leave the room. She emphasized the door as a place that marked transition.

Since that moment in class I have continued to ponder the door as a threshold experience. When one enters, one arrives as a person, as a subjective, individual self. Once in the room, one joins others and becomes part of a group. After a parent meeting or some other event, one returns home with new thoughts and impulses, in short, a different person. Parents can move from subjectivity to greater objectivity, a greater perspective when they walk in and out of a doorway to a classroom. The same holds true for the teacher, who *may see the world enter the room and then retain a breadth of understanding that is refreshing and new thanks to the parents who have visited.*

If the door is a significant demarcation of experience, how can we enhance the quality of the transition for parent–teacher interactions? It matters ever so much what state of mind we are in when we cross the threshold, even the ordinary ones of the classroom or the door to a home after a long day at work. Have we done some clearing of the day's events, processed our work experiences before entering the doorway? Alternatively, are we bringing an armful of baggage that we need to dump in the room? Have we thought about the substance of the evening ahead of time or are do we just rush in?

In regard to a class night, the teacher often does a great deal of preparation. It is seen as part of the job. Thus the state of mind and attentiveness to the moment may be heightened. The danger is more on the parent side, as many may come straight from work without dinner or any inner processing time.

Thus I recommend that meetings and class nights begin with transitional activities that help people "land," and that the threshold experience of walking through the door be extended to allow for personal transitions.

These transitional activities can include sharing from home life or work, singing, a game, a gymnastic activity, or anything that brings people together. The point is to find one another in the new space and leave the previous experiences of the day outside the doorway.

In our spiritual life there are also threshold experiences. These can occur when there is a crisis, a death in the family, an illness, or the birth of a child. These can pass as just a major event, or can be the impetus for life changes. What we make of threshold experiences is very much up to us. But in a meditative practice it is also possible to come to a threshold experience in which one leaves the world of sense perception and enters the spiritual world with one's inner being intact as opposed to drug induced states where that is not the case. Here it is also of vital importance to have some preparation ahead of time, or else the experiences in the spiritual world can be shattering to the soul. Fortunately the spiritual worlds have provided a helper for such circumstances, a Guardian of the Threshold, who can not only protect and guide, but also help determine when one is ready to cross the threshold. More on this subject can be found in the descriptions given by Steiner in How to Know Higher Worlds *and other books and lectures in which he has described the School of Spiritual Science.*

When one visits a Waldorf school, one often sees an administrator greeting children at the front door of the school. Then, upon entering the building, one sees teachers greeting and shaking hands with the children as they enter their classrooms. This is experienced as a joyful moment in the school day, yet with the consciousness of the doorway in mind, it has profound implications. The schoolroom today has its historical roots in the Academy, and the academy has its roots in the ancient mystery centers that existed in special places around the world thousands of years ago. These special places were sites where one could undergo a schooling of the inner life, an initiation. Sometimes lasting thirty years or more, the neophyte would go through elaborate stages of preparation and training, in which moral/spiritual development went hand in hand with academic education. Each stage of learning was a threshold, a crossing. When a teacher greets a child with a handshake at the door of the classroom, it evokes ancient traditions of learning thresholds.

The door of the classroom is the portal through which both child, parents and teachers pass. It marks the threshold of moving from the old to the new, from what we are to what we can become. It is an opportunity to leave our old selves behind and become someone new. It is a moment of passing.

The doorway of a classroom can be seen as simple lumber, nails, or mortar—an "it." Or a doorway can be crossed with devotion and reverence as a threshold experience, a moment of "I–Thou." It contains both the ordinary and the loftiest portion of human experience.

"I am the gate; whoever enters through me will be saved. They will come in and go out, and find pasture" (John 10:9).

Appendices

Parent–teacher Survey:
Letter to Parents and Teachers

Dear Parents and Teachers in Waldorf Schools,

You are being asked to participate in a survey about parent–teacher relations in a Waldorf school.

The information you provide will be used in writing my next book, *A Second Classroom: Parent–Teacher Relationships in a Waldorf School.* I hope the book will benefit new teachers, parents beginning the journey, and all those who want to examine how parents and teachers can best work together in the context of building a school community.

There are minimal risks in taking part in the survey as the use of participant names is optional and no respondent will be cited by name. If you provide your name and contact information (see questions # 19) it gives me the option of asking a few of you to participate in a follow up interview. Specific information gathered in the survey will not be shared with school administrators or any other party and the names of schools will be omitted in the book. Completed surveys should be returned in an envelope to the school office. They will then be mailed to me in a secure priority packet.

The survey takes about 10 to 15 minutes to fill out and participation is completely voluntary.

You may also leave any question blank if desired, but please answer as many questions as you can.

If you have any questions about the project please contact me at 603-283-2310.

If you have any questions about your rights as a research participant, you may contact Dr. Katherine Clarke, Chair of the Antioch University New England Institutional Review Board, 603-283-2162.

Thank you for your participation.

> Sincerely,
> Torin M. Finser
> Chair, Education Department
> Antioch University New England

TEACHER QUESTIONNAIRE ON PARENT–TEACHER RELATIONS RESEARCH PROJECT: THE SECOND CLASSROOM

1. Your Name (optional):

2. Age:

3. Gender: (circle one) female male

4. Years Teaching:

5. Present Role: (circle one)

   Early Childhood

   Class teacher

   Lower School Subject Teacher

   High School

   Administration

6. Years at present school:

7. Are you also a parent at the school? Yes No

8. Parent of alum of school? Yes No

9. Place in your family of origin? (circle one)

   only child   first-born   second   third   other

10. Which of the following do you most use to communicate with parents (may check more than one)

    ___ telephone calls; any restrictions?

    ___ letters; how often?

    ___ emails; any guidelines?

    ___ how many class nights per year?

    ___ how many parent–teacher conferences
        per year?

    ___ written progress reports;
        more then end of year reports?

11. On a scale of 1-5 please rank each of the above (5 as being most effective and 1 least effective. Put number to right of choices above).

12. What advice would you give a young teacher in establishing a good working relationship with parents?

13. What specific things can parents do for you that make you feel supported?
14. In which ways do you most need parent help?
15. Is there any difference in your interactions with fathers vs. mothers?
16. Do you have teacher's children in your class(es) and if so, what advice can you offer in working with the parents of those children?
   Are there reasons why you may be reluctant at times to receive input from parents?
17. What makes you pay attention to suggestions from parents? Do you listen to some parents more than others, and if so, why?
18. What are the greatest challenges you have faced in working with parents? Please list them briefly:
   1.

   2.

   3.
19. Has there been a particular incident in your parent–teacher relations that you would be willing to describe in an interview so that others might learn from your experience? This might have been a difficult situation that was resolved successfully, or a situation that became a conflict that needed the intervention of others.
   Yes   No
   If yes, please write your name and email address so you can be contacted for an interview:
20. Is there a topic regarding parent–teacher relations that has not been mentioned but deserves further inquiry?

Thank you for your help!

Parent Questionnaire for Parent–teacher Relations Research Project: The Second Classroom

1. Your Name (optional):
2. Age:
3. Gender: (circle one) Female Male
4. How many years have you been a parent at your present school?
5. How many children/students do you currently have at the school?
6. Have any of your children graduated 8th grade? Yes No 12th grade? Yes No
7. Your place in family of origin? (circle one)

        Only   first-born   second   third   other

8. On a scale of 1 to 5, please rank each of the following communication tools a teacher might use (5 being the most effective, 1 the least effective):

   ___ Phone calls from the teacher checking regarding a sick child or specific issue

   ___ Monthly letter to parents

   ___ Emails

   ___ Class nights

   ___ Parent–teacher conferences

9. What advice can you give a new parent in terms of establishing an effective parent–teacher relationship?
10. What makes for a successful parent meeting/class night?
11. What qualities in a teacher make for good parent interaction?
12. What do parents most need from a teacher in order to feel met and supported?
13. Is there a difference in terms of relating to your children's teacher(s) if one is a mother or a father? If so, please describe from one or more perspectives.

14. What are the greatest challenges you have faced as a parent in working with a teacher?

> 1.
>
> 2.
>
> 3.

15. Has there been a particular incident in your interactions with a teacher that you would be willing to describe in an interview so that others might learn from your experience? This might have been a difficult situation that was resolved successfully, or a situation that became a conflict that needed the intervention of others.

Yes   No

If yes, please write your name and email address so you can be contacted for an interview:

16. Is there a topic regarding parent–teacher relations that has not been mentioned but deserves further inquiry?

Thank you for your help.

Parent Survey: Question 9

What advice can you give a new parent in terms of establishing an effective parent–teacher relationship?

"Set up an introductory meeting and say hello at pick up or drop-off. Participate in workdays and offer support for tasks to be done at home or at school. Help your child bring their teacher flowers or goodies. :-) Make every effort to communicate quickly if anything comes up with the class or teacher—addressing issues early on builds trust and ensures that the issue does not escalate."

"Let the teacher teach—trust him/her. You entered a Waldorf system; let the experts to their thing. Don't approach in the morning before main lesson. Listen and honor the response when you ask a question. Don't try to change things—let the Waldorf curriculum work its magic."

"It is a partnership. A collaboration of love between the most important people in a child's life—the parents and the teacher. Being honest and open to communication, speaking through love with both parties, and holding the best interests of the child as the primary concern has been my favorite experience."

"Waldorf education is as much an education for your child as it is for you. Be open and transparent—it is a journey; always appreciate the moments, but keep the big picture in mind. With your teacher, share thoughts and observations, but also do not be overly sensitive (or critical) without allowing space and development. If you have a concern, express it to your teacher before you express it to the other parents."

"Be empathetic and forgiving of your teacher. Your child's teacher has much to contend with—lots of different needs and challenges by many children AND parents—and is human just as your child is. The best way to develop a long-term relationship with your child's teacher is to think of them and treat them as a colleague—one that you respect, honor, and admire. Trust will come in time and difficulties will inevitably come. So developing an open and warm-yet-professional relationship with your teacher in the very beginning will go a long way to the many years ahead of successes and growth opportunities."

"Ask questions as they arise. Don't ever feel like your question or concern is silly or unimportant. We have a long journey with our teachers, particularly in the Grades, and confronting questions and concerns is crucial for building a healthy long-term relationship with your teacher."

"Schedule time to speak one on one with the teacher that is not squeezed in with drop off or pick up to connect and establish how communication flows with the class, teacher to parent and parent to parent. Find out how to address grievances, questions, etc. This respects the teacher's time as well as your own. It's very challenging for a teacher to address specific questions while juggling students."

"Be open and honest always from the moment you meet. Address behavioral issues sooner, rather than later."

"Go to school events. Meet and talk with your child's teacher frequently, at pick up or whatever is least formal but convenient."

"Don't be afraid to advocate for your child. Your Waldorf teacher would rather know everything that is going on for the child in any sphere of his life."

"Give your child's teacher time to get to know your child. If you need to discuss specific issues, set up time to meet, rather than trying to "catch" a teacher at either end of the day. Keep an open mind and listen. Be your child's advocate, but remember you child's teacher is one too."

"Be honest with the teacher regarding your concerns about the potential shortcomings of the school, its curriculum (boy I wish I had spell check . . .), or how it might not meet your child's needs. I have found the teachers to be very understanding and appreciate the feedback. If they get defensive, then I would take this as a warning signal regarding the quality of the teacher."

"Take advantage of Parent–teacher conferences, letting the teacher know when there are personal issues going on for the child, discuss any problems that arise and don't assume that the teacher sees what you see."

"Find out which form of communication the teacher prefers and utilize that. Ask if the teacher has available times to meet on campus."

"Prompt, honest, humble communication."

"Be friendly, be available to volunteer, but give teachers space to teach. They know what they are doing, and are quite capable. Support at home is *key* to a child's success."

"Do your homework. I notice many parents frustrations are born from not actually knowing what to except from a Waldorf school— for example, not getting enough homework."

"Face to face interaction, honesty and transparency. Share with the teacher what your expectations are of them and what you want for your child."

"Wow, this either happens or it doesn't. If you find yourself with a teacher with whom effective communication isn't working, be brave and move your child to another school. Follow your intuition."

"Commitment, trust and communicate. Make a deep commitment to the teacher as a partner in raising your child. Value the commitment like you do your commitment to a spouse/partner or family member and continually work at the relationship. Consider them a fellow human being with a full spectrum of strengths and weakness but trust that they have your child's best interest at hand and they are doing their best and what they feel is right for the class as a whole. And your child."

"Don't hesitate to ask questions, ask advice and advocate for your child's needs. The answers may not always be satisfactory, but the only way the teacher will know what your child needs is to speak up. Share info about family history, background and culture, highlighting what is important—a second language and heavy emphasis on heritage culture, traditions."

"Listen. Your teacher almost definitely has seen more children in school situations than you have. Listen to what they have to say and really absorb and digest their observations and conclusions."

"Love, appreciate and *support* your child's teacher. They are not paid well and they have a huge amount of responsibility. I would bring mason jars of homemade soup to my daughter's teacher regularly. She was a single mom of two with a commute. Follow the rules. If there is a no TV policy, follow it. If the teachers ask you to pack wholesome lunches, do it. Your children learn by imitation, if you respect their teachers they will, too."

"An open line of communication and mutual respect are key in establishing an effective parent / teacher relationship. Address issues and/or concerns as they arise. As parents we are very protective of our children and, at times, we tend to make assumptions based solely on one-sided feedback we receive from our children. To forge a strong relationship between parent, teacher and child we need to approach any issues that may arise with an open mind. We must be willing to look at the situation from every angle and not jump to conclusions. In my experience, especially in the lower grades, I feel it is important to keep the teacher apprised of any changes or challenges that may be occurring in the child's home or social landscape. They say it takes a village to raise a child. This is our village and each of us plays a critical role in the development of our children."

"Be persistent. Never give up."

"I would recommend that new parents develop a relationship and direct communication with the teacher from the outset. At Waldorf you are (hopefully) in it for the long haul and therefore it is inevitable you will reach difficult junctures. A relationship that has been built slowly and over time will serve everyone when things get bumpy. I think it is important to develop a level of understanding that the teacher is very busy and ultimately very human. In my experience, parents who are drawn to Waldorf education are very idealistic—as are the teachers. There are positive outcomes and negative outcomes from this idealism."

"It is important that you bring all of your perplexities and concerns to your child's teacher. It is ideal if you can bring them in a questioning/questing sort of way, in a mood of exploring and willingness to learn. No question is too odd or ungainly; it gives the teacher help and info. If you can, as a parent, look further into the role of school for your child and see it as a schooling for you as a parent, that will help. There are a lot of beneficial things to learn that will really help your whole life. Try them out (even if they sound sort of odd to begin with). Also, if there is any way that you can know that your child's path is set up to re-trigger your issues from childhood and if you can get solid support (from a counselor, pastor, trusted friend) in dealing with what comes up for you, then your relationship with your child's school and teacher will go a lot better. There is no way for any Waldorf school to be perfect all of the time (even if that first visit to the kindergarten classroom seemed like heaven). If you can know this from the get-go, it will ease some of the upset that does come up at times. Forgiveness is a skill we all need to learn (and our kids need to see us learning it)."

"Believe in your own abilities as a parent when considering the needs of your child. Teachers have their area of expertise and can be immensely helpful, especially when your child needs extra help or struggling in a specific area, but you are the expert on your child. When you are confident in your own abilities, it is easier to accept advice as it makes sense to your child's needs."

"Try to attend meetings and participate in class events. I know this can be difficult. Both my husband and I work full time. It's not just your relationship with the teacher; it is also the relationship you have with the other parents at times. Many of our parents have become close friends."

PARENT SURVEY: QUESTION 10

What makes for a successful parent meeting/class night?

"Organized agenda, ideally with a handout listing important points about future events/needs from parents. Child care."

"Parent education. This can include hands-on experience with what the children are doing, conversation about the commonality and differences among parenting styles, and/or education about how the philosophies/techniques/curriculum meet the intentions of the education."

"A teacher who's not afraid to control the aggressive parents who sometimes take over making sure that their children get the same special treatment that they get at home."

"Order and someone with a highly developed ability to herd cats."

"I don't know...we have had three graduates after a lifetime in Waldorf and pretty much all Parent Meetings are terrible. The most successful has been when a teacher that is Waldorf Trained and works out of anthroposophy gives a talk on development."

"Food (just kidding). Time to share concerns in an open honest, supportive non-judgmental place."

"Agenda, good facilitation, good process, ending on time."

"If everyone comes... I think that parents nights should be mandatory. Provide child care. (Yes, even at night) the teacher or parent council rep should find out the best times for the most people to be able to show up."

"Having it on the weekend... weeknights are too difficult with bedtime/dinner and family activities."

"Full turnout of the parents. If only a few are there both parents and teacher have to rehash with non-attendees and the sense of sharing is limited. Then a bit of pedagogy especially looking ahead, some sharing of anecdotes and a limited amount of business planning."

"Attendance of many other families. A nice combination of class sharing and true dialogue with the parents. I wish more parent meetings were done over dinner or a glass of wine than in the classroom."

"Teacher brings specific issues they are currently dealing with in the class so parents can discipline or work on those issues at home, as well—child ends up benefiting from a unified front which makes everyone's jobs easier."

"Like anything in life, everyone wants to be heard and appreciated. There are many topics that can and should be broached as the years progress—some are simple yet important; some are controversial and will never be resolved. Regardless, the teacher's ability to hold a group of parents through the various discussions that occur during a class meeting in an open dialogue and respectful space is key to a successful meeting...and even successful group of parents. It is unfortunate but in this day and age our teachers need training in this area just as they need training on how to be teachers. If a teacher can work even half as well with the adults as they do with the students, the chances for a successful class with minimal attrition is high."

"Lots of details about what's happening in the classroom, explanations of curriculum, opportunities to look at artwork or lesson books, opportunities for the students to present what they've learned."

"Learning about an aspect of Waldorf philosophy and how the teacher related that to his or her class. Hearing how the class as a whole is doing. And seeing an example of what the class is work."

"Again, openness and honesty. Remembering that parents have different parenting styles and that one family's way of being is not necessarily the same as another's."

"Seeing a bit of what the children do in the classroom and having general questions about how the classroom runs. Hearing other parents' opinions and questions is really helpful too."

"Keeping the parents on track, not letting the talk drift off topic and lose the valuable time. Having parents respectfully listen when the teacher is speaking, and not chat with their neighbor."

"The most successful thing is good participation and a well prepared teacher. Dividing the meeting into equal parts parent education, learning about what the students are doing and having time to share. A very successful practice is having the parents do some of the activities from the class such as singing the blessing, doing a math exercise on the circle or playing a word game."

"Not too early—not too late—not too long! Well-established agenda. Personally, I do not want the entire meeting to be about how much help the teacher needs and all about signing up for every event of the year. I want more info about what is going on in the classroom—as the kids get in the older grades I want to know how they stack up to other kids their age and I want them to be ready to take and pass high school entrance exams (we don't have a Waldorf high school)."

"Parent meetings have been a disaster in our class. All *successful* outside meetings I have attended, whether at work or in support groups or community advocacy groups, there is a *structure* as to when and how often any one person can speak, and the group leader feels empowered to redirect or even stop a person from speaking if they so deem necessary. One example of a successful format (which I love) is to keep a list of all attendees, and for the group leader (the teacher in this case) to CALL on people "randomly" from this list until all attendees (over the course of several meetings, perhaps) have spoken, whether they chose to or not. People who "raise their hands" or just their voices over and over are bullies or know-it-alls, and the teacher would not tolerate outbursts from these kids in the classroom, so why should she tolerate this in adults? Teachers are afraid to offend parents, and potentially lose a student because of this. But if the blow-hard "More-Steiner-Than-Thou" parents are not corrected by the leader, then the less sure, less righteous parents may get the impression that silence equals consent by the leader, and pull their children from the school because of they don't like what the blow-hards had to say. Teachers need to *step up* and *be* the *leaders* to the adults just as they are to the children. This is how meetings are able to be successful: good leadership and clear, unbiased guidelines."

"Not what you are doing but Why."

"Humor and lack of anthroposophic dogma!"

"Organization, an agenda and timeliness."

"Less lecturing and more information as to what the children are doing. It's extremely difficult to get to these meetings so having them less frequently and more in depth is important to me."

"First the parents need to know there is a meeting well in advance so they can schedule for it. Second, the teacher must realize they are speaking with adults at this time and treat them as such. Third the teacher must be organized, perhaps have the agenda for the meeting written on the board so parents can see how much there is to cover and help stay on track."

"The best class meeting nights have been led by the teacher so the parents do not go off on their own individual agendas. The meeting agenda is clear and connects what the children are learning to the Waldorf philosophy. We love seeing how the development of the children connects with the curriculum."

"Participation by the parents, and take-home materials to reinforce what was discussed, so it doesn't get forgotten."

"Brevity, concise provision of information, and addressing all topics at hand. Making sure *all* parents are involved in the classroom needs (and not just those who willingly and regularly raise their hands)."

"The most important factor is a clear agenda and the ability to reel it back in when the meeting gets off track. Exercising mutual respect. I experienced parent meetings where issues that should have been dealt with on a one-on-one basis were called out in the middle of the meeting. I strongly believe in the philosophy of praise in public, correct in private. The class meetings should be an opportunity for us to all come together for the greater good of our children and not a venue for personal attack."

"Starting on time and as many parents attending as possible...keeping the business to a minimum leaving time for parent/teacher discussion about topical subjects."

"The teacher needs to have very good rapport with the parents. If that is lacking, then I think the teacher needs to work on that (in them and with the parents that cause "problems"). The teacher also needs massive amounts of tact and very strong crowd control skills. The best phrase I have heard is: "I would like to suggest..." This leaves each to their own reaction, but also gives the teacher the place to take the lead. If the teacher is a practicing anthroposophist (working on positivity, open-mindedness, and developing the ability to say "not I, but the Christ in me," and working with the spiritual world) then they have something to bring to the meeting that every single person is hungry for—caring and a deeper perspective. I think parents are often perplexed by their children and if the teacher can explain the curriculum (because they love the curriculum) and how it is just right for the age of the child, it really supports the parents. If all of this seems a bit much, then it is good for the teacher to have their mentor or another teacher be at the meetings (perhaps as a guest speaker on a topic of interest to the parents—i.e., Why do my kids hate homework when they used to love it, and what am I to do about it?). I think it helps a lot to have a getting to know each other activity at the beginning of the talking part of each meeting (sum up summer in six words, stand on an imaginary map and move around for every place you have lived since birth, or share what your child's eighth grade project is...). If there can be something artistic to start that is great—watercolor, eurythmy, singing—the arts are getting easily squeezed out, in some Waldorf schools. Anything a teacher can do to help the parents see the importance of art for the social, emotional and intellectual development of their child is important can go a long way in supporting the curriculum."

Parent Survey: Question 11

What qualities in a teacher make for good parent interaction?

"Authenticity in communication. Being open to frustration and not getting defensive. It is not about you; it's about the dynamic of the situation. Warm, inviting and encouraging. Being able to reach out right away when a problem is presented. Not waiting too late to communicate issues."

"A certain amount of softness to temper firmness, friendliness and knowledge.

1. Waldorf-trained
2. Works from Anthroposophy
3. Explains him- or herself
4. A sense of humor
5. Gives concrete advice when asked
6. Follow-through

"Open minded, good interpersonal skills, good listening skills, empathetic.

"Someone who responds to emails or a phone call in a timely matter. The teacher should have a personal voice mail. Not just one at the school, but their own at home also. I know that one of my son's teachers rarely if ever gets the messages I have left at home."

"Exceptional organizational skills; NVC background; an ability to receive parental emotion/fears without taking it personally, and clear frequent communication."

"Availability, Honesty, Listening, showing patience with a parent who is stressed, worried, etc. about their child's success or lack of working on solutions, offering options."

"Professionalism, some teachers are too personal and although they think it makes them more approachable it doesn't, it sets up a dependency on either side depending on the teacher. Waldorf teachers also need to find a way to be more down-to-earth, not in a Waldorf cloud."

"Being engaged! When I was looking into Waldorf last year my husband and I attended a parent and teacher "interview" with two teachers. (We were looking into Waldorf for both of our kids in two different grades). One of the teachers knitted the entire meeting! Our son that would have gone into her class is still at his present school. Not a good time to multi-task... Not a good parent interaction. A teacher should stay focused on what will benefit the child and how to meet the child's needs as an individual. I like to see a teacher excited about an opportunity to have time with me to ask anything they need to that will benefit my child. Engaged—focused—excited."

"A teacher who can show s/he understands a child's strengths and challenges, by giving specific examples. A teacher who sits back and listens. A teacher who can make parents feel as if s/he is a partner with the parent."

"Humility. Patience in understanding that most negative emotions are based in fear, and often effectively abated by offering comfort appropriate to context. Having a sense of center and boundaries, and having kind simple ways to make these boundaries clear, and to enforce these boundaries. A sense of empowerment and support from the faculty body and leader such that the teacher need not live in fear of repercussions from setting said boundaries."

"Flexibility, tolerance, warmth, intelligence."

"Obvious love of student, obvious love of teaching (particularly Waldorf education), respect, listening, sense of humor."

"The teachers we have interacted with have been willing to listen and have an insightful perspective about our children. The most successful interactions have been when we feel heard and understood and leave learning something about our children and what the Waldorf education is providing for them. Having written that, I realize the traits are; the ability to listen, convey understanding, experience and an added bonus is an enthusiasm for teaching and being part of our child's development."

"Willingness to talk on the phone or in person as much as needed."

"Sincerity, approachability, genuine care for and familiarity with my child, availability, sense of humor, being down-to-earth and realistic regarding daily life. Also, if we were to be welcomed into the classroom for some kind of a 'parent work day' it would be so beneficial in building a parent–teacher relationship and partnership."

"Openness, lack of defensiveness, honesty, compassion, desire and intention to do what is truly the best for the class and the individual child. Education, experience is important but does not come before centeredness. Teacher's need to constantly work on becoming the best human they can be. The teacher-student relationship is also reciprocal."

"An openness and willingness to communicate directly, listen and be honest. It really goes back to the idealism; we are there because we are idealistic but we are also very human. I have found a good rule is to never assume—just ask. This goes both ways with the parent and teacher. I think this is especially important in a Waldorf community where there can be a lot chatter and spin amongst the parents. Waldorf education (especially for parents who are new) can feel very overwhelming and obscure. I really appreciate it when our class teacher explains what she is doing in a simple and straightforward manner with the focus on how it supports our children."

"If a teacher is practicing anthroposophy (ideas about this listed previously) this can help. I think it often helps if a teacher has children of their own (they are then lots more humble about what it is like for parents and can share some of their own stories at times). Also, if the teacher has some understanding of non-violent communication a lot of hard places can be avoided. The book "Practicing Non-Violent Communication" by M. Rosenberg is easy to read and has lots of real life examples (including many of Marshall's own interactions [failed and successful] with his own family members). If the teacher has unlimited time (Ha!) and can always meet with parents and answer questions the parents don't have to let things build until they just leave the school in a huff. Two parent conferences a year are often not enough. If the teacher understands the deeper reasons for aspects of the curriculum then they can share about that and often smooth feathers, say by putting the issue in perspective (I remember one parent being upset that the 2nd grade teacher was making their kid into a Christian. The 2nd grade teacher said "just wait—next year they will be Jewish and then the next year Norse/pagan...etc.). I also think there are times when a teacher needs a huge and very strong connection with their own angel. That there are times when teachers are challenged (and these are heartbreaking) and if the teacher does not have strong support from within and also from peers, the injustice is too hard to bear. I suppose a connection with the Christ being and the ability to bear suffering with grace is a skill that will be called upon if one takes up the path of teacher in a Waldorf school (that should be covered in Teacher Training, actually I think there ought to be a whole year devoted to teacher/parent relationships—I am glad you are writing a book about the topic)."

PARENT SURVEY: QUESTION 12

What do parents need from a teacher in order to feel met and supported?

"Parent–teacher conferences. Make needs for classroom clear; utilize class parents and parent-council representatives for communication with class and/or leadership bodies of the school."

"Transparency into the teaching and classroom management of teacher. Parents need to know that challenges and conflicts are being addressed and that resolution does not exist until the teacher and the parent believe it does."

"Honest communication and non-judgmental listening. I want to hear where my child needs support and improvement, not just what a shiny star she is. Waldorf teachers have a wealth of information that can help me in my parenting and I want to learn it. Raising a child is not always sweetness and light though. How do we handle the tough times?"

"Being open to implement new ideas that are different to them or that they have not had training in."

"Teachers need to have Awareness and be sensitive to spiritual/religious orientations."

"Communication. I need to feel heard. I am paying several thousand a year! I want to be heard. I think that more social opportunities might help."

"An understanding that the teacher truly "knows" their child and holds their best interests at all times. Clear communication about their child's progress and what the class as a whole is doing."

"Quick responses to questions that are clear and not emotionally charged."

"Acknowledgement that parents are/have been heard."

"Compassion, to be heard, teacher can repeat what you are saying, Teacher remembers your concerns and tells you that he or she remembers."

"Honest communication. Assurance that they hold and love your child as much as you do. Empathy for the lack of support the parent is receiving outside the school. Assurance that the teacher is holding the highest and best image of the child & recognizes their worth."

"Reassurance. That their child is doing well and is finding their way and that they see who their child is and is becoming."

"Firmly believe that a happy, excited and growing child and class is what parents need most. Secondary, is to feel kept in the loop about what is happening in the classroom and any parent expectations so parents can plan accordingly."

"Sensing interest/understanding of one's child. Fairness."

"To know their concerns have been heard and will be addressed."

"Not just listening, but hearing."

"Open to listening to parent concerns with empathic disposition."

"Just to feel that they are being heard and to be educated on what we don't understand, which in my experience Waldorf teachers do an amazing job at."

"A parent needs to genuinely know that their teacher is listening to their concerns and won't immediately become defensive. A parent doesn't want to feel that if they bring a concern that their teacher will "black ball" their child."

"The knowledge that the teacher actually knows your child, is aware of his struggles (and the families struggle's as well) and communicates frequently about problems.... and successes (I would love to hear more of that on a more frequent basis). Regular, short emails are helpful to make a parent feel secure in what is going on at school and provides a different perspective that can help ward off problems when a child tells a "crazy" story about what the teacher did today. It's amazing the different stories that can be told about the simplest incident. A child can easily make the teacher look unfair, unresponsive, etc. More communication the better."

"Clear concise information about the activities/issues/events going on at school and maybe why they do it. I have one teacher that rarely sends any info to us about anything or with little notice and one that e-mails us daily going on and on about health issues and detailed breakdown of daily activities yet doesn't call us when needing last minute requests or to let us know our child needs to bring something to school the next day, it is just in an e-mail which we don't read at night."

"Availability and approachability. Knowing that a teacher is available for evening phone calls or after school meetings without it seeming like a hassle is important. Parents know teachers are overworked and underpaid—we don't like to impose. But a teacher who makes it clear (in words and deeds) that they are available for questions and conversation makes parents feel much more met and supported."

"Parents need to feel that teachers care, that they see and can articulate issues, that they have reflected on a plan to deal with issues and that their concerns and comments come from a sound understanding of the relevant issues. Authenticity is also very important."

"Recognition."

"I am going to answer this very much from my own personal experience. I really appreciate the breadth of experience my son's class teacher has—experience in life and her many years of teaching both in public and Waldorf schools. She can look at things from a broader perspective as well as through the Waldorf/anthroposophic lens. I don't know if we could have stuck it out without her wisdom and openness. My son has challenged her. Our family is far from perfect; we don't fit the classic Waldorf family mold. Yet, she has been open and willing to work with us. When we hit rough spots, I feel like I can really talk to her. This connection and trust has been built slowly, over time."

"1. A listening and compassionate heart. 2. Secure and mature emotional health. 3. Never taking a tone of defensiveness. 4. To always look for solutions, not blame. 5. To guard the confidential information of all at all times. 6. A bright and quick sense of humor. 7. The demonstration of deep care/affection for the students."

"A sense of competence, professionalism, warm-heartedness."

"Honesty even when it's uncomfortable. Clear expectations communicated to all. A clear picture of what's going on in the classroom socially as well as academically. Requests for input/help from the teacher vs. feeling closed off from the day-to-day. Creative partnering for developing solutions to problems and to enrich the curriculum or relationships."

PARENT SURVEY: QUESTION 13

Is there a difference in terms of relating to your children's teacher(s) if one is a mother or a father? If so, please describe from one or more perspectives.

"I have found that teachers expect the mothers to be more involved in the school and children's activities. This is annoying to me as a mother, but is a societal problem and not really a parent–teacher problem. This may be slowly changing and teachers should encourage this change."

"I don't think so, not from our experience. It has more to do with where one's mind is—nothing to do with gender."

"Men simply garner more respect from teachers, so fathers are able to have more impact."

"As a father, I don't feel that there is any difference in terms of relating to our teacher."

16 "Certainly. Communications are always different from a male/female perspective and also from the perspective of the gender of the child and the teacher."

"I think it is different in each circumstance but on the whole generally one of the pair is more concrete/goal focused and the other more process touchy-feely."

"Speaking as a mother, I don't think so."

"Well in the case of my husband and me, I am the one who drops off and picks up and so I interact differently and more often with the teachers and classmates, too. We try to share the parent–teacher nights, especially now with 2 kids in school. And my husband has been around Waldorf education his whole life (mother was a Waldorf teacher) so it's not new to him and he is less emotional about all the beautiful ceremonies because to him they are just the right way of doing things. And I agree!"

"I think the differences are more driven by the mother/father rela-tionship and/or broader dynamic than any specific gender difference."

"At least at our school we have learned how to appeal to mothers when we market our school. Most of the dads I know at our school are going on faith that Waldorf education is good for their chil-dren—trusting that their wives have made the right decision. Since I am the mother and from one of those families, I'll defer to the men to help define what they need in order to understand and buy-into

Waldorf education. But the one thing I can say is if we are going to expand this movement nationally, we have got to start speaking to the men—utilizing the many scientific studies that have been done in the last 10 years that have explained brain development in a child and how and why Waldorf education is better fitted for children than other types...and how it can provide them with a greater chance of academic and other success in the long-run."

"I am a single parent so I'm not sure. I think it can be different relating when a parent works or doesn't. For the ones who don't and are at school before and after class a lot of information gets passed and shared between parents. For those who work they are often out of the loop except for teacher emails and parent meetings."

"I don't really see life in these terms. I think it's more about personalities then gender."

"Of course, because my husband communicates with each of our children's teacher much differently than I do. We appeal to different sides of our children's teacher. I like supporting the teacher to make teaching easier, my husband stays on top of the academics."

"I can't answer for my husband. I take care of the children more than he does. I drop off and pick up. I take care of everything so of course I have more interaction with the teacher. I go to all of the parent/ teacher conferences. I don't think there is a difference because of our gender but more because of the role we play in our children's lives and the structure of our family unit."

"Certainly. As a full-time working mom, it is much easier to relate to my son's female kindergarten teachers. They both were in the same situation of balancing working full-time with the demands of running a household."

"In general mothers tend to be more concerned with the child's social and emotional wellbeing. Father's tend to concern themselves more with academic achievement and being prepared for the future."

"Perhaps. Communication with fathers tends to be briefer, more direct, more action-oriented or task-oriented. Teachers rely on parent volunteers in pretty gender-defined roles. Moms are asked to cook, drive, craft, clean, stage-manage, sew. Dads are asked to build, drive, coach, etc."

"My experience has been that the mothers lead the family into the Waldorf world—it is often an emotional decision for them especially in the early years. Fathers follow but need proof of concept or they will veto. Seasoned Waldorf fathers seem to be the most reasonable—they are supportive but don't get pulled into the drama. (I am really, really generalizing.)"

"My husband doesn't really have anything to do with school in general. When he does I know it is important to him to feel welcome and to have some guidance if he has not been to school for a long time. For me, I'm always there so it is very different."

Follow-up Interviews

These comments from a parent and two teachers in follow-up interviews point out the ways in which the relationship between a teacher and parents can either break down or work well.

When the Relationships Break Down

A. An Example from a Parent

> "You asked whether the nature of our parent relationships with teacher/school is different for father than for mother. I've had to think quite a while on my answer. Initially, my thought was around what areas my husband and I would bring our concerns: academic challenge vs. social dynamics; physical activity vs. the arts; etc. It may be possible to divide some of these topics of concern into areas that have a stereotypically quantitative-thinking-masculine basis or qualitative-feeling-feminine basis. In any case, if the issue addressed were quantifiable it was (not surprisingly) easier to address. But the softer issues, those that are more qualitative than quantitative have been harder to resolve.

Regarding our relationship with our Waldorf school. The circumstances that lead us here (a place of profound disappointment) are not unique to families in Waldorf schools—as long as there are people there will be relationships that lie somewhere on the continuum between richly rewarding and woefully dysfunctional. What is different in a Waldorf school as opposed to other schools, however, is an expectation that both the student–teacher relationship *and* the supporting relationships *around* the student–teacher relationship will be functional (if not optimal) and durable. Longevity and commitment is part of what we've sought.

When we chose Waldorf education for our children, we entered into a committed relationship with the school and a particular lifestyle. The expectations are higher in committed relationships—for both parties. As parents we expected our feedback to be received respectfully. Granted, formal feedback was not sought. And perhaps the absence of that invitation to provide formal feedback speaks to a lack of a plan for how to integrate it. In any case, there was an expectation on our part that given the depth of commitment we had made to a Waldorf education, that there was equal commitment on the part of the teacher and school to work with us toward the best possible outcomes, in all the many layers of relationships that come with being part of a Waldorf community.

When our eldest child was in the younger grades, we were advised that the teacher/parent relationship should be nurtured and cultivated. We would benefit in later years when our child was an adolescent and would likely rebel against both teacher and parents. We accepted that as good advice, and supported the teacher in every way we could. When the relationship between our adolescent student and his teacher became strained—perhaps a little earlier than is typical—we approached the teacher with our concerns. Our feedback was not accepted as credible. It was rejected. The teacher simply did not accept our feedback. We took our feedback to the administration. It was not welcome. There were repercussions for our bringing negative feedback."

B. FROM A BEGINNING TEACHER

As told in an interview the job application process for this new teacher went well, the class teacher job was formally offered, and the new teacher was invited to a "meet and greet" session with parents. This is when things began to unravel. Instead of being just a social event, some of the parents began to treat the event as a second interview. They asked pointed questions, including some that were borderline from an HR perspective. One parent did a personal investigation, including checking with the teacher's family members, and one father even called the new teacher to say "you are strange and weird." Some families started a petition of non-enrollment and a majority signed it based upon the inappropriate "meet and greet" event. The very existence of the class was called into existence and the new teacher had to wait most of the summer to hear if the job was still available.

In hindsight, it turned out that there were some deep seated issues parents had with the school and that they latched on to the new hire as a point of leverage to exert influence on school decision makers. They used the "trump card" of enrollment to be heard.

When Relationships Serve the Needs of Parents and Teachers

"Communication is essential. It, of course, matters ever so much who one is talking to, but I have learned that one needs to communicate as things are happening. If too much time goes by, parents can wonder, "When did this start? Why did the teacher wait so long to tell us?" Parents should not have to wait for a regular parent–teacher conference to find out what is going on. Teachers often want to have all the information together before talking to parents, but sometimes that takes too long...touch in with parents as things are happening. Involve them early on.

One also has to choose the best time of day for all concerned. If one is hungry or tired, communication will not go so well. One has to be in a good state of mind. A teacher can always say, "Let me think about this and I will get back to you tomorrow."

Sending letters home in lunch boxes is no guarantee they will arrive or be read. Send an email to alert parents that material is coming home. Likewise, when parents tell me things on the playground, I ask that they follow up with an email, as I cannot remember every person who volunteers to drive for a field trip, for example.

Regarding Moms and Dads

Dads tend to be less communicative. When a class night has mostly dads, there is less conversation. They ask fewer questions. They seem to want the essential information and then go home. Of course, moms can be like that, too, especially those that have heavy work schedules. In general, it is hard to work with disconnected parents.

A teacher needs to encourage feedback, even critical feedback. "I need to know." Also, a teacher should ask for mentoring on the parent–teacher relationship from experienced teachers....a mentor should attend class nights.

Parent work is the hardest work you do. There are no parent internships to prepare the new teachers. It is on-the-job learning.

Student Experience

Takken Wish
Evolving Consciousness
Remembering Mr. Atkinson

Mr. Atkinson was not happy with us. In front of the classroom he stood, his cheeks red, the puffs of hair over his ears more wild than usual. Once again we, his seventh grade Social Studies class, had raced through a series of multiple choice questions, as well as a whole chapter of American history, without retaining anything.

"But I asked you to read the chapter!" he shouted. "That means read it closely! Then, after you've read the chapter closely, answer the questions carefully!"

The lesson had begun like every lesson with him—with page numbers on the blackboard and a worksheet waiting on each desk. The whole hour class was to be used for this work. We'd learned quickly, though, that we did not need the whole hour to do well on such an assignment. We could read the questions, identify the key words, then skim the chapter for the answers without really reading, and be done quickly, often scoring perfect scores, all the while leaving plenty of time to horse around with friends. We knew once we finished he had nothing else for us to do.

"You're lazy kids," he shouted. "Don't you care about actually learning?" Then he began asking us random questions about the chapter. Though we'd answered all the questions on the worksheet correctly, we could not answer his direct questions. Finally he sat down at his desk, shaking his head, disgusted with us.

Some students weren't bothered at all by his disappointment in us. They went on as usual, chatting with friends, their moods cheerful as ever. After all, we'd secured our A grades by acing another worksheet, and now had time to goof off.

I was bothered, though, and I felt guilty for not really trying. I knew we'd cheated by not really doing what was expected of us, by not really doing what was right. At that time, I blamed myself for taking the easy road rather than being driven to really learn that history. Looking back, with several years of teaching under my belt, I feel that Mr. Atkinson was just as responsible for our behavior, if not possibly more responsible. I say this because he is the one who provided an activity that was easy to complete without any real thought. To do this once might have been forgivable. Mr. Atkinson, though, gave work like this day after day without seeming to question his teaching methods. Basically, instead of teaching us American History, he was teaching us how to cut corners and how to complete work without having to break a sweat. We were making A grades in his class, after all, so how could he argue that we needed to change?

As I look back at that class now, I think about two main points. First, I want to have activities that require involvement from my students. I want the work to matter to them. Also, if my students are not responding to my lessons the way I want, then I need to analyze myself and my lessons to figure what I need to do differently so as to get the results I want. Mr. Atkinson did not change his behavior. Since he didn't change, it is ridiculous that he criticized us for not changing. Good teachers must be able to reflect back on lessons that did not work as planned and figure out what could have been approached differently. Likewise, teachers need to be able to analyze classroom successes with the aim of understanding why the lesson went well.

If something does not work as I want it to in my class, I never want to pin that failure on my students. If I ever do actually think that the problem is not with me but truly with the students, then I believe that it would be time to ask for outside help, such as from parents or ideas from other teachers.

Zoe Aaronson

I started kindergarten when I was barely four years old. I was given special dispensation to start early because my parents and the administration felt I was intellectually advanced. I was also given permission to attend full day even though only half days were offered.

I still recall my first day of class quite clearly. I remember I was looking forward to starting school. I figured the teachers had heard about me and I wanted to show off what I could do. I sat up front so I could be close to the teacher. There were many teachers in the classroom that day because they wanted to evaluate all the children. We were given many small tasks to complete. A teacher would come by and ask questions and make notations on a clipboard. I only remember three of the tasks. The three tasks were: read a book, write my name, draw a picture of an animal.

For the first, I was to read a small book that involved Dick and Jane and seeing Spot run. I read it in seconds. I thought it was easy and stupid. I was used to trying to read through *Winnie the Pooh* on my own at bedtime along with other books. So, when a teacher finally came by I was occupying myself. I was scolded for not being engaged in my schoolwork. I argued that I had completed my work. I wasn't to be believed. I quickly reread the book to prove I had done it. The teacher couldn't believe her ears and had me read it again. She jumped to the conclusion that I had previously encountered the book and thus must have memorized it. She retrieved another book for me to read. I read it just as quickly as the first. There was a mini conference between the teachers. They got me adult books to read. I read those as well, but didn't know all the words. I thought they seemed comforted by that. I don't think they knew what to do with me. There was a small argument on whether or not to give me the next task or have me wait for the other students to finish. They decided to give me the next task.

For this second task I was to write my first name. I wrote my full name. I then proceeded to write every other word I knew. I quickly ran out of room on my piece of paper. When I asked for more a different teacher was in for a surprise. I had to rewrite some of the words for her and explain what they meant. This teacher had assumed that I was copying them from somewhere and didn't really know the words. Yet another discussion between teachers ensued. Eventually, it was another teacher who insisted that I WASN'T writing with assistance or by trickery that got everyone to withdraw. They weren't convinced, but they were done arguing. I found out that teachers wouldn't take a little kid at her word. I was also surprised that someone hadn't told the teachers I was coming.

Finally, I was given the only other task I have memories of. I was to draw a picture of any animal I wanted. I could tell they were hoping it would occupy me. So, I drew as carefully and as slowly as I could. I started by using my ruler to draw lines on my paper. This drew comments that I was supposed to be drawing an animal not lines. I explained I wasn't finished. First, I had to draw where it lived. After the lines, which were supposed to be the bars of a cage, I drew in vines, flowers, and trees. When I was finished with the background I thought it was magnificent but, it probably looked like a trellis with flowers. Then I started drawing in birds flying around. When asked what it was I said it was a menagerie. I even showed the teacher I could spell it. The teacher asked me how I knew to spell it and I told her it was just like a menage a trois. She gasped and went running off. She came back with another teacher and told me to repeat what I had said. When I said it again they both had a giggling fit. When yet another teacher came over to see what the fuss was about she freaked out when she was told. Everyone calmed down when they figured out I could say it, but didn't know what it meant.

At that point I was attracting too much attention. The other children were distracted from their work since they would try to see what I was doing or ask me questions. I was moved to a desk in the back right corner of the room. I was scooted far enough back so that the other students couldn't turn around and talk to me. I was exiled. I hated school. The teachers were unkind and wouldn't believe me. The other kids got me in trouble by talking. There were too many stupid rules and it seemed everything I did was a mistake. I wasn't learning anything, and I definitely wasn't having any fun. This is how I felt about school all the way through.

Now, I know Steiner was right when he stressed the importance of the first day, first lesson. The first day should be about welcoming the children and awakening in them a desire to learn and grow. Every day should be like that. Teachers should care about students personally and not just intellectually. As teachers we must see and work with the whole child. Also, children can only benefit from their parents being more involved in the classroom and having an open dialogue with the teachers. Expecting the teachers to know about me and know I was coming may have been slightly presumptuous of me as a child, but it would have paved the way for me. A child's education really is a collaboration.

I have also learned that the things adults say and do, inside a classroom or outside of it, really can have an affect on a child that may last their entire life. Sometimes teachers need to look back and remember what it is like to walk in a child's shoes. It may help us make better choices. I know remembering affected my choices. I found Antioch because I felt there was more to education than what I knew. There is more to education than academics. Each child is more important than the ABC's. Learning and growing is a part of life and we should have fun while we're doing it together.

TILDEN LEONARD-FRITZMEIER
EVOLVING CONSCIOUSNESS: REFLECTION PAPER
September 20, 2013

My memory of that day is cloaked in a too-bright white light. The kind of light that pierces your nerves like a cold metal dentist's tool coming across a hidden cavity. I craved the calming natural light of my old classroom. I wished I could close my eyes and return to the comfort of Mr. Meade's room and the familiar faces of my friends. Instead I was in this still-unfamiliar room, filled with faces of classmates I still barely knew. I stared down at the blank piece of paper on my desk as it reflected the harsh florescent light back at me. I could feel myself getting more anxious by the second.

Mrs. Hall stood at the front of the room. She was a tall woman in her early sixties with short gray hair and glasses. She spoke, "one...two....three." All at once, my classmates and I flipped our papers over. Now in front of me appeared a page full of multiplication problems. We had two minutes to complete as many of the problems as we could. My heart started racing and my mind went fuzzy. I wanted to cry.

At the end of two minutes I still had a number of unfinished problems in front of me but I knew the ones I had managed to answer were correct. I had always been proud of my ability to do all of my times tables accurately. Math had been a source of confidence building for me. I was a shy child and often doubted my abilities in school. I had even suggested to my parents and teacher that I be held back after the first grade. They had assured me that I was ready to move on, but my fears of being less-than continued. Math had helped me overcome these fears. I knew it was something I was good at. Until now.

The day after taking the timed math test, Mrs. Hall announced that based on the results of the test, the class was going to be divided into three sections; above average, average, and below average. She started with the names of children who had done exceptionally well. My name was not called. My name was not among the list of "average" children either. My ideas of myself being less-than were then confirmed as I heard Mrs. Hall call out my name. I was below average.

After sending my brothers and me to a Waldorf school for four years, my parents fell into some financial difficulty and could no longer afford tuition. I spent my fifth grade year at home with my brothers. My parents were unable to keep up with home schooling and most of the year was spent exploring outside, making up games and playing music. After this "adjustment" year, as it has become known as in my family, I knew it was time to go back to school. I missed learning and being around kids my age. I was scared but I was ready. I began my sixth grade year as the new kid at Wakefield Elementary.

Having received a Waldorf school education as well as a public school education has given me an interesting perspective, which I have come to appreciate. Although that day in sixth grade truly scarred the eleven-year-old me, the twenty-six-year-old me, studying to become a teacher, is grateful for the experience. I have seen a number of interactions between adults and children that remind me of my painful memory. It seems that something is lost on the journey to adulthood that causes one to forget their child selves. One of my goals as a teacher is to never forget that I still am that scared child, at a new school, in an unfamiliar situation. I want to create, for my students, the kind of nurturing and supportive environment I was surrounded by at the Meadowbrook Waldorf School. I do not want my students to ever feel inferior to their classmates or unsupported by their teacher, the way I did at eleven years old.

I think my experience will be beneficial not just in my relationship with my students but with their parents as well. Having a public school background will allow me to ease the worries of parents who may be new to the Waldorf school system.

My goals for teaching seem simple and intuitive and yet I know I will be working on them for the rest of my life. I want to teach the whole child. I want every student I teach to love to learn and to learn to love. I want to create an environment in my classroom in which no child ever feels "below average."

NINE LEVELS OF ESCALATION

1. HARDENING

Positions some-
times harden and
clash

Occasional glitches
and spasm

Awareness of the
tensions that exist
causes spasm

Conviction that
tensions can be
resolved through
talking

Parties and
functions not yet
entrenched

Cooperation (still)
stronger than
competitiveness

2. DEBATE AND POLEMICS

Polarization of
thinking, feeling,
will

Either/or thinking
(polarized

Tactics: pretend to
argue rationally;
verbal violence

Speeches to an
"audience": scor-
ing points via third
parties

Temporary group-
ings from around
certain stances

Discrepancy
overtone–undertone

Fighting for domi-
nance (Transaction
Analysis model)

Oscillation between
cooperation and
competitiveness.

3. ACTIONS, NOT WORDS

Talking no longer
helps, so actions
are needed.
Strategy of the fait
accompli.

Discrepancy
between verbal and
nonverbal behavior;
nonverbal behavior
dominates.

Danger of misinter-
preting actions.

Pessimistic expec-
tations rooted in
suspicion accelerate
the conflict.

"Group skin"; pres-
sure for conformity;
roles crystallize.

Empathy is lost.

Competitiveness
stronger than
cooperation.

4 IMAGES AND COALITIONS

Stereotypical
images; clichés in
relation to knowl-
edge and abilities;
image campaigns,
rumors.

Parties manoeuver
each other into
negative roles and
fight those roles.

Wooing supporters;
weakness leads to a
need for support.

Self-fulfilling proph-
ecy through fixation
on images

Covert provoca-
tion that is difficult
to prove; snide
remarks, irritation.

"Double bind"
through paradoxical
orders.

5. LOSS OF FACE

Public and direct personal attacks; moral integrity is lost.

Staging ritual unmasking activities; exposure leads to disillusionment; works retrospectively.

Image: angel–devil, Double.

Disgust, casting out, banishing.

Loss of external perspective; isolation in the "echo cave."

Ideology, values, principles.

Striving for rehabilitation.

6. STRATEGIES OF THREAT

Spiral of threats and counter-threats.

Triangle of threats; correlation demand/punishment/potential punishment; credibility through proportionality.

Locking in oneself and each other "trip wires."

Manoeuvering oneself into compulsion to act; loss of initiative

Stress increased through ultimatums and counter-ultimatums; scissor effect.

Acceleration.

7. LIMITED BLOWS

Thinking revolves around "inanimate objects."

Human qualities no longer valid.

Limited destruction as "appropriate response" (avoidance of excessive counterblows).

Reversal of values and virtues into their opposites; relatively small damage is considered a "benefit."

8. FRAGMENTING THE ENEMY

Bringing about total breakdown of the enemy system.

Destroying vital system factors to make the system manageable.

Isolating "front fighters from their hinterland."

9. TOGETHER INTO THE ABYSS

No way back.

Total confrontations.

Destruction of the enemy, even at the price of self-destruction.

Enjoyment of self-destruction, provided the enemy will not survive.

Willingness to cause severe damage to the environment of successors through one's own downfall.

Chart designed, in gratitude, after Friedrich Glasl, *Confronting Conflict: A First-Aid Kit for Handling Conflict*, Hawthorn Press, 1999.

Reading the Face

by Norbert Glas

To form a judgement about the system of cavities in the middle part requires us to consider important detail. An unbroken curve, covering about a third to a quarter of a circle, is a promising one. However, it should also have cavities that are deep enough. If both of these requirements are present (fig. 33), this frequently indicates a sick feeling life, which can also indicate a significant relationship to musical experience. Organically, such forms usually reveal good circulation and a strong heart. It is clear that the strength in people who are artistic is bound to be anchored in the middle part, just as all the emphasis falls on the rhythmic system.

Divergences from this ideal form exist everywhere, of course. Indentations toward the back appear especially often. These are sometimes so strongly in evidence that the outer furrow, which belongs to the antihelix, is pushed aside. Ears like this tell us that these are people who live very strongly in their feeling life and are strongly engaged in their own feelings. Outwardly, they can seem very reserved. They live more in themselves, as a snail that likes best of all to creep into its shell. They have a difficult nature, yet they can make extraordinarily valuable contributions if they can master the overly abundant

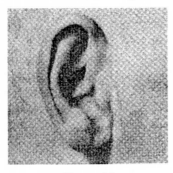

Figure 33

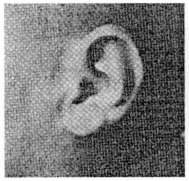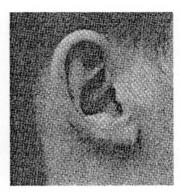

Figures 37, 38, and 39

forces in their middle organism. They may also become very taciturn people and appear mysterious. (fig. 37).

When these characteristics are exceeded, they appear in the form of pathological conditions. This can happen when the feeling life is directed more toward the metabolism and becomes "entangled" there. People may become prisoners of their lower organization, especially when it remains sluggish and weak; poor digestion and hardening are signs of this. Such people become pathologically melancholic. This reaches the point of true melancholy. Those suffering from this are forced, in their feeling life, to participate so intensively in the sluggish behavior of their intestines or liver that they no longer want to do anything; they sink into themselves, and all they can feel is earthly weight and its suffering. This can be expressed in a certain way in the ear (fig. 38); the lower part of the curve in the middle area is exaggerated, and points more in a downward direction, as the illustration shows. This ear belonged to a patient who suffered for a long time with such intense melancholy that it called for a lengthy stay in an institution.

We see a contrast to this in the kind of changes that appear when the curve enclosing the cavities has either been shifted or bent, or when the whole area is too small and much too flat. The ear of a child with special needs, whose trouble is located very strongly in the feeling life, is an example. In this case (fig. 39), all that is

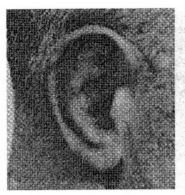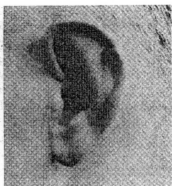

Figures 40 and 41

retained of the circle is only about an eighth, at most, and at the other end it is, instead of being curved, a bit snapped-off at an angle.

The ear of a man who for many years suffered from aortic stenosis is very constricted, with little depth to the cavities (fig. 40 and 41). This is a good illustration of how weakness in the circulatory system, in the case of an organic heart defect, can be mirrored in the "heart region" of the ear. Here you can also see that the breathing and the blood organization have to work together closely. It seems relatively straightforward to sort out the different parts of the upper or middle ear. But to see clear divisions in the lower section proved very difficult for a long time. Eventually, though, we discover obvious distinctions in the bottom third, as well, and it can be seen as a mirror of the situation in the metabolic-limb organization.

Where the individuality of a person is concerned, it means a great deal if there is a clear division of the three systems, both from the points of view of the body as well as of the soul. A blurring or dissolving of boundaries can prove serious. Like two gatekeepers, to use an image, even if it strikes some people as too bizarre, there are two lumps of cartilage in front of the entrance into the underworld of the metabolism; these two guardians themselves belong to this third realm. We are talking about the tragus and the bit on the other side, the "antitragus." They present an image of the functioning of the lymph and glandular system. We might be able, too, to see from

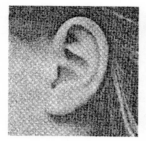 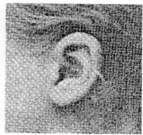 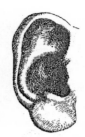

Figures 42, 43, and 44

the way these are formed how dynamic the person's fluid organization is. If this is healthy, there should be a certain distance between these two points—that is, they should not be too far apart or too close together (fig. 42). A good example of a narrow construction is of the ear of a developmentally challenged child who became much too fat, and whose tendency in this way must be attributed to a glandular disturbance. The striking narrowness of the lower break in the auricle (*Incisura intertragica*, fig. 43) is also due partly to the fact that the tragus and the antitragus have come too close to each other. At the same time, we often encounter a thickening on the upper third of the ear on the outside, toward the back, where there is a particular indication of the relation to the form-giving forces. People such as this, with a tendency to dispense with form and grow fat, reveal a phlegmatic temperament.

It is easy to find the opposite to this. This is when the tragus and the antitragus are too far apart (fig. 44). Here there is a predominance of the risk of too much entering the glandular system and possibly overwhelming the person. This occurs for example in people who suffer from an overactive thyroid; they are excessively excited, their whole metabolism goes too fast, and they readily lose weight and grow very thin. They are often exaggeratedly sanguine in temperament and are ruled by unconscious forces of their metabolism (fig. 45). The boy shown earlier, in figure 17, can also be seen as an example of this. His ear is a clear example of the tragus and antitragus being too far apart. Thus far, he shows no signs of

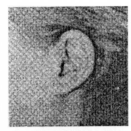

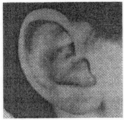

Figures 45 and 17

any problem with his thyroid, but his whole character reveals that he is driven by instincts, with the unconscious part of his being rising from his lower organism. His temperament shows a marked sanguinity; he is fairly imaginative and extremely talkative. His urge to take things that do not belong to him indicates that he cannot control his unconscious (fig. 17). As the form of his ears shows, there is no distinct division between his middle and his lower organism, which explains why he does things that are not under the control of his conscious self. A well-formed tragus and antitragus that are at a harmonious distance from one another can be observed in people who have great skill in their hands and fingers. Moreover, their character shows an immediate willingness to help others.

The next form to be distinguished in the lower ear is the gap dividing the tragus and the antitragus. This gap, its width, depth and shape, will of course always have a close connection to the two "gatekeepers" to the lower region. This is obvious, because the individual functions of the metabolic system are very closely connected. However, the incisura intertragica is more a picture of the deeply buried processes in the organism; rather, we have to think of the phenomena related the processes in the intestines and kidneys insofar as they are linked more to the transformation of substance than to the transformation of the processes leading to the excretion of waste matter. The gap can form a beautifully harmonious line, which everybody will immediately recognize as such (fig. 46); going from this regular form, there are all the other gradations in the way of a form which becomes increasingly wider and indicates a lively capacity for transformation in the metabolic system (fig. 44); while a narrowing, as seen in the previously mentioned child, draws attention to a decided weakness operating even deeper within the organism than only in the field of the glands. We mentioned this in particular before (fig. 47).

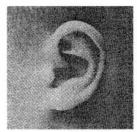

The third area in the lower third of the ear, which is also of special importance, is the ear lobe. It is the living expression of the inner force that builds up the human organism, its ability for constant regeneration; and the ability to reproduce also partly belongs here. There is actually a mirroring here of the polar opposite forces to those that are expressed in the back part of the upper ear.

Figures 46 and 47

That is where we see the disposition of all the form forces to a hardening and also the effective functioning of the senses. These forces of rigidity can, in the case of illnesses such as gout, not only take hold of the upper body, but become visible as hard little knots just in this particular place and stem from little crystals consisting of salts of uric acid. Look at the ear lobe in comparison. It is totally free of gristly substance, and is the softest part of the outer ear. In our body the will is anchored predominantly in the metabolic system, which creates its mirror image especially expressively in the ear lobes. Ear lobes can be very different. Those that are harmoniously rounded (fig. 48) are roughly a third of the ear in size. We have also to mention the ear lobes that have a slight point at the bottom, and these give not so much a picture of the total will forces as a picture that emphasizes the force of sexual reproduction. The custom of wearing earrings has to do with this side of the metabolic organism; it is intended to increase awareness of the power of procreation (fig. 49).

Broad, almost square ear lobes are a remarkable phenomenon, and their owners usually have strong metabolic systems; while their metabolic strength usually provides them with a good basis for a

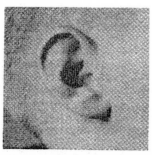

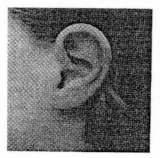

Figures 49, 50, 51, and 52

strong will. People who are typically choleric often show forms like this (fig. 50).

It is of decisive importance to everybody what kind of will organization they have. Have they come down to Earth showing that they want to work to the full extent of their capacities or will they have reservations regarding what they do? The kind of will-power they have is characterized right from the beginning of life, by which of these directions is typical of them. They will be more inclined to be active, to "go for it," or they will prefer to let things take their course without their having to do anything about it.

If we want to classify people in this way, we could also say that one sort develops a strong will, showing an urge to do things from their own initiative, whereas the other sort seems to have been born with a weak will. The ear lobe is significant for showing this strength or weakness. In fact the kind of ear lobe that has a loose bit hanging down shows the push to be free, the force of free will, whereas the ear lobe that is a continuous part of the ear is a sign of a weakly disposed will system. The best thing to do is to line up both kinds, the kind that hangs loose and the kind that has grown together with the rest of the ear, in one picture (fig. 51 and 52). People with loose-hanging ear lobes are prepared to use their legs and feet to move forward with determination. People who possess a more grown-together kind seem to find it far more difficult to use their limbs to move freely on the Earth.

All that we have said in this connection has nothing to do with what an individual can work to achieve, despite a tendency that was originally different. We have finally managed to find three different parts in the lower ear, too, that mirror the metabolic system: the area of the tragus and antitragus as a picture of the lymph and glandular function, and also altogether as a token of the liveliness or weakness of the metabolism; the area of the gap tells us something about the nature of the work going on in the intestines and kidney system in the transforming of substance; and the ear lobe, which becomes an image of the mobility of the processes in the lower organism, and again reminds us emphatically that the will is based in the metabolic-limb system.

∽

This section of the appendices is from the book *Reading the Face: Understanding a Person's Character through Physiognomy* by Norbert Glas (Temple Lodge Press, 2008); used by kind permission of the publisher.

Roadblocks to Listening

There are nine roadblocks to effective listening and communication. Some you use consistently; others you may use with certain people or in particular situations; others you don't use at all. Everyone uses listening blocks sometimes, but it is helpful to be aware of your personal blocks and to consider their impact on effective communication.

Comparing

Comparing makes it hard to listen because you are always trying to assess who is smarter, funnier, more competent—you or the other. Some people focus on who has suffered more, who has bigger problems. While someone's talking you think to yourself: "Could I do that well?... I've had it worse, he doesn't know what bad is... She's so much more together than me." You can't let much in because you're too busy worrying about how you measure up.

Rehearsing

You don't have much time to listen when you're rehearsing what to say. Your attention is on the preparation and crafting of your next comment. You look interested, but your mind is somewhere else as it remembers a story to tell or thinks of a point to make.

Mind Reading

The mind reader is busy trying to figure out what the other person is really thinking and feeling. "She says... but I'll bet she's really thinking..." The mind reader is interpreting and analyzing, and typically pays less attention to words than to interactions and subtle cues, in an effort to see through to the "truth."

Judging

Negative labels or judgments have enormous power. If you pre-judge someone as incompetent, uncaring, or stupid, you don't have to pay much attention to what they say. You've already written them off. A basic rule of listening is that judgments should only be made after you have heard and evaluated the content of the message, and then the judgment should be considered tentative and subject to modification.

Identifying

When you identify, you take everything a person tells you and refer it back to your own experience. A parent wants to tell you about their child's tantrums, but that reminds you of the time little Stephanie laid on the floor and screamed for an hour. You launch into your story before the parent can finish. Everything you hear reminds you of something you've felt or done. There's no time to listen and empathize or to get to know the other person because you're so tied into your own experiences.

Advising

You are always ready with help and suggestions. You don't have to hear more than a few sentences before you start searching for the right advice. However, while you are thinking up solutions you don't hear the feelings; and you diminish others' personal power to solve their own problems. Advice is best given after you had fully heard another, and generally when you are asked.

Diverting

When you divert, you typically change the subject, distract. or humor the other person. You tend to divert when you get bored or uncomfortable with a conversation. You may try to joke with the other person to help avoid the discomfort. Or you may completely change the subject to distract attention from the uncomfortable issues. "Let's not talk about..." "Did you hear about..." "I've got a funny story about..." All these responses serve to divert attention from listening to the concerns of another.

Being Right

Being right means you have the correct answer and you'll go to great lengths not to be wrong. Your convictions are unshakable. You often warn, order, admonish, or command others to adhere to your beliefs; or you may find that you preach or moralize—anything to try to let the other see how right you are. "Do this... or else; you should...; you need to...; you had better..." This tactic produces defensiveness and resistance.

Placating

"Right... right... I know... yes... really... it'll be OK..." You want to be nice and you want people to like you, so you agree with everything. You may be half-listening, but you're not really involved. You are not tuned in to what's being said.

Which of these blocks apply to you? In this space list the roadblocks that seem typical of the ways you avoid listening to parents?

_____

_____

From Barbara L. Wolfe, Virginia G. Petty, and Kathleen McNellis. Special Training for Special Needs. Copyright 1990 by Allyn and Bacon. Reprinted with permission.

Why on Earth?

by Signe E. Schaefer

Since Rudolf Steiner's day, and most especially in the last two decades, brain research has become ever more sophisticated, and many differences have been revealed between male and female brains. For example the male brain is eleven to twelve percent larger by weight than the average female brain, but certain areas, such as the deep limbic system with its relationship to feelings and their expression, are proportionally larger in female brains. The area to do with mathematical ability appears to be larger in male brains. Men tend to process things better in the left hemisphere, which is the area of logical, rational thinking, while women use both the left and right hemispheres equally well and have a larger corpus callosum, which plays a role in the rate of transferring data between the right and left hemispheres. Men use mainly the left hemisphere for language, while women again use both sides. It is interesting to question whether research like this can provide a background to communication patterns noted in Deborah Tannen's popular book *You Just Don't Understand*. She points to the phenomena that women tend to use language to share intimacy, to offer support, to build consensus and community, while men are more likely to speak in order to solve problems, to offer advice, or to establish their identity. Painfully well-known patterns of miscommunication might perhaps be alleviated if women and men could acknowledge genuine differences offered by our different bodies.

Of course, research into differences can also make us very uncomfortable and we may fear how it could be misused to further oppress. Equality of opportunity is essential, and worth upholding in every imaginable setting, but this cannot really be done by ignoring differences. Clearly brain size, in relation to gender, is not a significant factor in intelligence, any more than average differences in body size govern essential human experiences; and yet a male or female brain may offer different inclinations for our Earth learning, just as the rest of the physical body does. And, of course, we must still consider the interplay within every woman and man of feminine and masculine qualities, and also the role of socialization in gender identity. Always we return to the undivided "I" inhabiting the body, learning, balancing, and deepening as a human being through what the body offers.

The influence that a male or female physical body exerts on our earthly lives is illuminated by the experiences of transgendered people. Whether because of ambiguous anatomy or an inner sense of "being in the wrong body," ever more people (or at least more are speaking out) seem to feel they do not fit neatly into the categories of male or female. This particular, and often very painful, destiny has come into discussion, study, and social activism as people who do not easily identify with either gender have begun to articulate their experiences. Their own stories, their struggles for recognition and rights, and also bestselling books like Jeffrey Eugenides' sensitive novel *Middlesex*, offer testimony to the reality of a sense of self not bound by the gender of the physical body, but that still may long for the experiences that one gender or the other, or both, might offer. Through reading and also through my limited acquaintance with people who have had sex-reassignment surgery, I have become aware of the profound sense that many have felt since childhood of not identifying with the gender of their bodies. By going through the long and painful process of making this change, it seems almost as if they are experiencing two lifetimes in one, at least from the perspective of gender. Their "I" clearly experiences something not comfortable, perhaps not anticipated, about the physical body they were born into, and through the medical procedures they endure, they may achieve some semblance of remedying this situation. Others, who opt not to have surgery, may also find a new acceptance of, and relationship to themselves through their transgender identity.

From Signe Eklund Schaefer, Why on Earth? Biography and the Practice of Human Becoming, *pp. 23–24 (used by permission).*

Core Principles of Waldorf Education

by PSC of N. America (January 2013)

Waldorf Education can be characterized as having seven core principles. Each one of them can be the subject of a life-long study. Nevertheless, they can be summarized in the following manner:

1. Image of the Human Being: The human being in its essence is a being of Spirit, soul, and body. Childhood and adolescence, from birth to twenty-one, are the periods during which the Spirit/soul gradually takes hold of the physical instrument that is our body. The Self is the irreducible spiritual individuality within each one of us, which continues its human journey through successive incarnations.

2. Phases of Child Development: This process of embodiment has an archetypal sequence of approximately seven-year phases, and each child's development is an individual expression of the archetypes. Each phase has unique and characteristic physical, emotional, and cognitive dimensions.

3. Developmental Curriculum: The curriculum is created to meet and support the phase of development of the individual and the class. From birth to age seven the guiding principle is that of imitation; from seven to fourteen the guiding principle is that of following the teacher's guidance; during the high school years the guiding principle is idealism and the development of independent judgment.

4. Freedom in Teaching: Rudolf Steiner gave curriculum indications with the expectation that "the teacher should invent the curriculum at every moment." Out of the understanding of child development and Waldorf pedagogy, the Waldorf teacher is expected to meet the needs of the children in the class out of his/her insights and the circumstances of the school. Interferences with the freedom of the teacher by the school, parents, standardized testing regimen, or the government, while they may be necessary in a specific circumstance (for safety or legal reasons, for example), are nonetheless compromises.[1]

5. Methodology of Teaching: There are a few key methodological guidelines for the grade school and high school teachers. Early Childhood teachers work with the principles appropriate to the way in which the child before the age of seven learns, out of imitation rather than direct instruction.

6. Artistic metamorphosis: the teacher should understand, internalize, and then present the topic in an artistic form.[2]

7. From experience to concept: the direction of the learning process should proceed from the students' soul activities of willing, through feeling to thinking. In the high school the context of the experience is provided at the outset.[3]

8. Holistic process: proceeding from the whole to the parts and back again, and addressing the whole human being.

---

1   A note about school governance: while not directly a pedagogical matter, school governance can be an essential aspect of freedom in teaching. Just as a developmental curriculum should support the phases of child development, school governance should support the teachers' pedagogical freedom (while maintaining the school's responsibilities toward society).

2   The word *artistic* does not necessarily refer to the traditional arts (singing, drawing, sculpting, etc.), but suggests that, like those arts, the perceptually manifest reveals something invisible through utilizing perceptible media. Thus a math problem or a science project can be just as artistic as is storytelling or painting.

3   This mirrors the development of human cognition, which is at first active in the limbs and only later in the head.

Use of Rhythm and Repetition

Relationships: The task of the teacher is to work with the developing individuality of each student and with the class as a whole. Healthy working relationships with parents and colleagues are also essential to the wellbeing of the class community and school.

Spiritual Orientation: To cultivate the imaginations, inspirations, and intuitions needed for their work, Steiner gave the teachers an abundance of guidance for developing and inner, meditative life. This guidance includes individual professional meditations and imagination of the circle of teachers forming an organ of spiritual perception. Faculty and individual study, artistic activity, and research for additional facets of ongoing professional development.[4]

---

4   There are four basic rhythms with which the Waldorf teaching works. The most basic of those is the day/night (or two-day) rhythm. Material that is presented on a given day is allowed to "go to sleep" before it is reviewed and brought to conceptual clarity on the following day. A second rhythm is that of the week. It is "the interest rhythm" and teachers strive to complete an engagement with a topic within a week of working on it. A paper that is returned to the student after more than a week will no longer be interesting to the student. The only interesting thing will be the teacher's comments, but the topic itself is already past the "interest window." A third rhythm is that of four weeks. A block, or unit of instruction, is usually best covered in four-week periods. This life rhythm can be understood in the contemplation of feminine reproductive cycle, for example, and can be said to bring a topic to a temporary level of maturity. The last of the pedagogical rhythms is that of a year. This is the time it can take for a new concept to be mastered to the degree that it can be used as a capacity. Thus a mathematical concept introduced early in third grade should be mastered sufficiently to be assumed as a capacity for the work at the beginning of fourth grade.

Bibliography

Appelbaum, Maryln S. *How to Handle Hard-to-Handle Parents.* Thousand Oaks, CA: Corwin and AYI Publishers, 2009.

Barnes, Henry. "The Third Space," Waldorf Online Library (waldorflibrary.org), Aug. 2003.

Brüll, Dieter. *The Mysteries of Social Encounters: The Anthropsophical Social Impulse.* Fair Oaks, CA: AWSNA, 2002.

Buber, Martin. *I and Thou* (tr. by R. G. Smith). New York: Macmillan, 1958, 1987.

Cunningham, John. *Compassionate Communication.* Nevada City: The Center for Nonviolent Communication, 2008.

Erikson, Erik H. *The Life Cycle Completed* (extended version). New York: Norton, 1997.

Finser, Siegfried. *Footprints of an Angel: Episodes from a Joint Autobiography.* Great Barrington, MA: Lindisfarne Books, 2012.

Finser, Torin. *Finding Your Self: Exercises and Suggestions to Support the Inner Life of the Teacher.* Chatham, NY: AWSNA, 2013.

———. *Initiative: A Rosicrucian Path of Leadership.* Great Barrington, MA: Lindisfarne Books, 2011.

———. *Organizational Integrity: How to Apply the Wisdom of the Body to Develop Healthy Organizations.* Great Barrington, MA: Lindisfarne Books, 2011.

———. *School as a Journey: The Eight-Year Odyssey of a Waldorf Teacher and His Class.* Hudson, NY: Anthroposophic Press, 1995.

———. *School Renewal: A Spiritual Journey for Change.* Great Barrington, MA: Lindisfarne Books, 2001.

Glas, Norbert. *Reading the Face: Understanding a Person's Character through Physiognomy.* London: Temple Lodge, 2008.

Glasl, Friedrich. *Confronting Conflict: A First-Aid Kit for Handling Conflict.* Stroud, UK: Hawthorn Press, 1999.

König, Karl. *Brothers and Sisters: The Order of Birth in the Family* (rev. ed.). Edinburgh: Floris Books, 2012.

Lawrence-Lightfoot, Sara. *The Essential Conversation: What Parents and Teachers Can Learn from Each Other*. New York: Ballantine, 2003.

Lievegoed, Bernard. *The Battle for the Soul*. Stroud, UK: Hawthorn Press, 1993.

Prokofieff, Sergei O. *The Occult Significance of Forgiveness*. London: Temple Lodge, 2004.

Schaefer, Signe. *Why on Earth? Biography and the Practice of Human Becoming*. Great Barrington, MA: SteinerBooks, 2013.

Sheehy, Gail. *Passages: Predictable Crises of Adult Life*. New York: Ballantine, 2006.

Steiner, Rudolf. *Calendar of the Soul* (tr. by H. Pusch & R. Pusch). Hudson, NY: Anthroposophic Press, 1988.

———. "Community Building." New York: Anthroposophic Press, 1942.

———. "Credo" (tr. by L. Monges). *Proteus Quarterly*, vol. 1, no. 1, spring, 1950.

———. "Credo" (tr. by A. Anderson). *Towards*, vol. 1, no. 4, 1979.

———. *The Four Sacrifices of Christ*. New York: Anthroposophic Press, 1981.

———. *The Four Seasons and the Archangels: Experience of the Course of the Year in Four Cosmic Imaginations*. London: Rudolph Steiner Press, 2008.

———. *Secret Brotherhoods: And the Mystery of the Human Double*. London: Rudolf Steiner Press, 2004.

Stengel, Richard. *Mandela's Way: Lessons on Life, Love, and Courage*. New York: Crown, 2009.

Tannen, Deborah. *You Just Don't Understand: Women and Men in Conversation*. New York: Quill, 2001.

Williams, Oscar (ed.). *A Little Treasury of American Poetry: The Chief Poets from Colonial Times to the Present Day*. New York: Scribner's, 1952.

CPSIA information can be obtained at www.ICGtesting.com
Printed in the USA
BVOW02s1024090315

390879BV00003B/145/P